Alfie

Alfie

The Life and Times of Alfie Byrne

TREVOR WHITE

PENGUIN
IRELAND

PENGUIN IRELAND

UK | USA | Canada | Ireland | Australia
India | New Zealand | South Africa

Penguin Ireland is part of the Penguin Random House group of companies
whose addresses can be found at global.penguinrandomhouse.com.

First published 2017
001

Set in 13.5/16 pt Garamond MT Std
Typeset by Jouve (UK), Milton Keynes
Printed in Great Britain by Clays Ltd, St Ives plc

A CIP catalogue record for this book is available from the British Library

ISBN: 978–1–844–88424–7

In memory of Tim White, 1976–2017

'If one awoke a Dubliner in the middle of the night,
and asked him the name of the Lord Mayor,
the chances are that he would mutter,
without opening his eyes, "Alfie Byrne".'

Irish Times, 3 November 1956

Contents

CONTENTS

The Freedom of Dublin

1882	Charles Stewart Parnell	Politician
1882	John Dillon	Politician
1902	John Redmond	Politician
1906	Douglas Hyde	President
1908	Richard Croker	Politician
1908	Hugh Lane	Gallery Founder
1923	John McCormack	Tenor
1932	Lorenzo Lauri	Papal Legate
1935	John Lavery	Artist
1946	George Bernard Shaw	Playwright
1953	Seán T. O'Kelly	President
1975	Éamon de Valera	Taoiseach and President
1975	John A. Costello	Taoiseach
1984	Maureen Potter	Entertainer

Since the year 1876, the Freedom of Dublin has been given to eighty-one people. These fourteen played a part in the life of Alfie Byrne.

1. Not to be Poor

'The greatest of our evils, and the worst of
our crimes is poverty; our first duty – a duty
to which every consideration should be
sacrificed – is not to be poor.'

George Bernard Shaw

Dublin was an Irish village, a Viking town and an English city. In the eighteenth century, some people called it the second city of the British empire, but that claim was always more impressive than accurate, rather like Dublin's conversation. An English actor, Samuel Foote, once said that he didn't know what the beggars of London did with their cast-off clothes until he saw the beggars of Dublin.

After the Act of Union, when the parliament on College Green achieved the ignoble distinction of voting itself out of existence, Dublin was politically castrated. In the nineteenth century, the heart of the city – the area governed by Dublin Corporation – became a refuge for the victims of famine, and the middle classes fled to suburbs like Rathmines, Pembroke and Clontarf. By the 1880s, Dublin had the worst urban adult mortality rate in the United Kingdom. Seán O'Casey's neighbours bought the cheapest tea and the cheapest fat, 'and waited for unsold bread to grow stale [so] that they might buy that cheaper, too'.[1]

The year 1882 saw the birth of Éamon de Valera, who

would become Ireland's most influential statesman; of James Joyce, who would become its greatest writer; and of Alfie Byrne, who was the most popular Dublin-born politician of the twentieth century. They all made a singular impression, but one of these men is now forgotten. This is the story of his life and times.

Alfred Byrne was born on 14 March 1882. The second of eight children, he had one sister and six brothers. His childhood home was at 36 Seville Place, a five-room terraced house in 'the workers' parish of St Laurence O'Toole'[2], where the north inner city meets the docklands. The house was demolished long ago, and we know little about the boy's early years, but O'Casey described the streets around there as 'long haggard corridors of rottenness and ruin'.[3] One of Byrne's younger brothers died as an infant. Another died at birth.

Byrne had tangled roots, like many Dubliners: town and country, Catholic and Protestant.

His father and grandfather were born less than a mile from his own birthplace, which allowed him to claim that he was a third-generation Dubliner. His mother, Frances – who was known as Fanny – was the granddaughter of Colonel Dowman, a Protestant soldier in the British army who had lived in Cork. Alfie was named after his mother's older brother, Alfred, who died at the age of thirty that same spring.

Byrne's father, Tom, worked in Dublin port, just as his own father had done before him; he was variously described as a ship's engineer, a docker, an engine fitter and a ship's pilot, and the last printed reference to Tom Byrne described him as 'shore engineer to the Dublin Port and Docks Board'.[4] He saw the cargo of the world arriving in Europe's largest village. There is no evidence that he ever enjoyed much comfort, and in 1895 he lost his job in the port for engaging 'too successfully in trade union organisation'.[5] As a fugleman for higher pay and more rights, he overstepped the mark at a time when organized labour was struggling to assert itself in Dublin.

As a result of this indignity, the family moved to an even smaller, two-bedroom house at 28 Lower Oriel Street, and two of the boys, Lar and Alfie, had to leave school to find work in order to support their parents and six younger siblings. At the O'Connell School on North Richmond Street, run by the Christian Brothers, Alfie was briefly a contemporary of James Joyce, and of Seán T. O'Kelly, who would go on to become something of a political nemesis. But now, his formal education came to an end. He was thirteen years old.

Leaving school at such a young age was not unusual at the time, and Byrne quickly found his feet. Within a few weeks he was selling programmes outside the Tivoli Theatre on Burgh Quay, and serving an apprenticeship as a mechanic in a bicycle workshop on Dawson Street. The business was owned by Charles Findlater, a scion of the well-known Dublin grocers, and his partner, a man called Martin, whose wife, Emmy, was a sister of Fanny, Byrne's mother.

As the birthplace of the pneumatic tyre, Ireland had a central part in the cycling craze then sweeping the world. On Dawson Street – just down the road from the grand official residence he would occupy as Lord Mayor – Byrne worked on some of the earliest safety bicycles, and later in life he would pride himself on the fact that he always carried out running repairs on his own bicycle. At a dinner for the motoring industry, Byrne spoke about earning his first half-crown as a wheel-builder. Years later, the *Sunday Chronicle* summarized his reverie:

As he built those cycle wheels years ago, Byrne often glanced from the little workshop windows and admired the Lord Mayor of the day; driving grandly in the historic Dublin mayoral coach from the Mansion House, which stands at the top of Dawson Street. Young Alfie never even dreamed then that he would himself drive in that same coach to welcome to Dublin the representative of the Pope . . . or that he would be elected the record number of eight successive times to the wearing of the heavy gold chain with its seventeenth-century William of Orange medallion, which had been worn in the past by such mighty men as Daniel O'Connell.[6]

In the spring of 1900, the ageing Queen Victoria made a visit to Dublin. When the Lord Mayor, Thomas Pile, proposed a formal welcome to the queen, thirty-two members of the City Council agreed with Pile; twenty-two disagreed. A young Dubliner called W. T. Cosgrave condemned the result of the vote in a letter to the *Irish Independent*: 'It should be remembered that within three years of her majesty's accession . . . the population of Ireland was nine million. Now it is only four million.'[7]

The news of the monarch's visit came as a shock: the city had only three weeks to prepare. A mock castle gate was hastily erected on Leeson Street Bridge, so that the queen could make a dramatic entrance into *her* city, and the visit was a festive occasion, with Union Jacks fluttering on rooftops and gates. But the jollity was not universal. W. B. Yeats derided those Dubliners who welcomed Victoria, while his great love, Maud Gonne, offered a trenchant critique of the 'Famine Queen', who had taken 'a shamrock into her withered hand'[8] to recruit Irish soldiers to fight for the British army in the Boer War.

Alfie Byrne came of age two weeks before the queen's arrival in Dublin. There is no record of his position on the visit, although we know that he later held Queen Victoria in high regard. In 1931, while showing journalists around the Mansion House, he proudly pointed out a large portrait of her. Like most constitutional nationalists, Byrne wanted a Dublin that was dignified, independent and friendly to London. This streak of Anglophilia would make him an object of suspicion for a generation of radical nationalists.

The census of 1901 revealed that Dublin had 290,638 inhabitants. On census night, Byrne was living with his parents and six siblings at 28 Lower Oriel Street. By that stage his father had found work again, as an engine fitter in the port. Alfred Byrne described himself on the census form as a 'grocer's assistant'. More precisely, he was working as a barman in an early house up the road from the family home.[9] The owner was a veteran publican called Tom Heagney, from Tullamore.

In his youth, Byrne did not join a debating society, the traditional training ground for aspiring politicians. He joined a public house. A journalist later observed, 'It was there, serving behind the counter, that [he] learned from his customers of politics and made his first essays in tactful pacifism, for dissension was then bitter between the Unionists, the Home Rulers, and the Republicans.'[10] Byrne also learned about the mechanics of power and influence in a community: how to flatter and win trust; how to tell a story; how to settle arguments; how to exude authority. There were other subjects on the curriculum, but these were probably the most important.

After a few years working near the port, Byrne left Oriel Street to manage a pub called Cosgrove's on Chancery Place, in the shadow of the Four Courts. There he lived alone in a room above the bar. Half a century later, the Lord Mayor received a letter from Mary Louise Cullen, 'the little girl' who had once lived in a flat beside the pub: 'I recall you quite vividly, you always were so good humoured, my dear father liked you, and mother.' Cullen remembered Byrne shepherding his flock at closing time: 'Now then gentlemen please, time's up!'[11]

Like many young men, Byrne idolized Charles Stewart Parnell, whose downfall at the age of forty-four was the defining political drama of the late-Victorian era in Ireland. One of James Joyce's first poems, 'Et tu, Healy?', was about the nationalist hero, and he once described himself as the Parnell of art. Byrne, for his part, remained faithful to the Home Rule legend. Many years later he would demand, and secure, a state commemoration for the centenary of Parnell's birth.

The party that was formed in Parnell's image went to war against itself, and while it eventually reunited under the Parnellite John Redmond in 1900, its MPs soon became all too comfortable. In *Vivid Faces*, R. F. Foster writes that Redmond was 'scornfully regarded by most young radicals, who believed that he and his parliamentary colleagues lived an indolent and corrupted life among the fleshpots of London'.[12] Back in Dublin, the Irish Parliamentary Party became notorious for doling out patronage and fixing appointments at grassroots level. Railing against jobbery and 'West Britonism', Sinn Féin politicians presented themselves as reformers and as the true representatives of Irish nationalism. They promoted teetotalism and often attacked publicans, who were well represented in the Irish Party.[13] So, too, were slum landlords. When an inquiry revealed that sixteen members of the City Council – the Corporation's elected assembly – owned eighty-nine tenements and second-class houses, it merely confirmed a widely held suspicion.

At the same time, new forces were emerging in Irish society. The Gaelic Athletic Association (GAA) was weaning Irish people away from 'foreign games', and the Gaelic League tried to promote the Irish language. The work of its founder, Douglas Hyde, complemented that of William Butler Yeats, Lady Gregory and John Millington Synge, who effectively forged a new national literature in English. The Abbey Theatre, which was founded by Yeats and Lady Gregory, would later become the first state-funded theatre in the world. But in addition to the public success of the Abbey, the GAA and the Gaelic League, there was subversive mischief to be had in student societies, agit-prop theatre groups, vegetarian restaurants, volunteer militias, Irish-language summer schools and radical newspaper offices.[14]

Poverty is an enemy of childhood. For some who survive it, an impoverished childhood creates a radical imperative *not to be poor*. As George Bernard Shaw put it, this is the 'duty to which every consideration should be sacrificed'. Alfie Byrne could not afford the idle pastimes of youth. While there is evidence that he played soccer with a club called Strandville, he was not a man for vegetarian restaurants, he did not speak Irish, and he had no interest in liberal intellectuals.[15] However, he was intrigued by politics, and his curiosity was encouraged by Tom Heagney, who would later become his father-in-law. Heagney was a cute country publican in Dublin – a type still prominent today – and a supporter of the Irish Party.

In 1908, Byrne went into business for himself, purchasing the Verdon bar at 37 Talbot Street. In the 1930s, a newspaper report claimed that the price was £500.[16] Becoming a publican was a natural move for an ambitious young barman, although it is unclear how he came by the money. Was Tom

Heagney perhaps involved? In any case, having come from nothing, Byrne was now, at twenty-six, the freehold owner of a going concern.

Over the next eighteen months, in addition to running the pub, Byrne served as treasurer in the local branch of the United Irish League, a grassroots organization linked to the Irish Party. This was an orthodox step for a go-ahead publican. Even before the franchise for local elections was expanded fourfold in 1898, grocers and publicans were heavily represented among the City Council's members.

On 10 April 1910, Byrne married Tom Heagney's only daughter, Cissie, in the Church of St Laurence O'Toole on Seville Place. (He was proud of belonging to the parish of St Laurence O'Toole. For the rest of his life, even when he moved to the southside, he told people, 'I'm a Larryer.') Byrne described himself on the marriage certificate as a licensed vintner. That summer, he told his new wife that he wanted to run for Dublin City Council. Tom Heagney was delighted, but there is no record of Cissie's response. She was a private, rather proud woman. Many years later, a rumour would emerge that Cissie had been a barmaid before she became Mayoress. It was not well received in the Mansion House. The Lord Mayor arranged for a firm denial to be printed in a local paper.

> The Lady Mayoress wishes to make known to her friends that at no time was she engaged in business, as stated in an English newspaper. Her father was owner of a licensed premises at North Wall, and another at Oriel Street, in which the Lord Mayor (Mr Alfred Byrne) at one time acted as manager. She became his wife shortly after leaving school, at which time he was conducting a licensed business of his own in Talbot Street.[17]

In December 1910, Byrne was formally selected by the United Irish League as a candidate in the North Dock Ward, at that time the biggest working-class district in the country. This was his chance – but, according to one account, he nearly chickened out. On 6 January 1911, the *Evening Herald* claimed that he was pulling out of the race. Was it second thoughts, perhaps, or a domestic crisis? The report is unclear. In any case, the very next day the paper revealed that the publican had reconsidered his decision. He would, after all, contest the election.

Public meetings were held to support the candidate, with two former Lord Mayors of Dublin, Councillor Lorcan Sherlock and J. P. Nannetti MP, appearing as star attractions. Nannetti said of his protégé, 'Mr Byrne is charged with the crime of being a young man, but it's young, energetic, active young men such as Mr Byrne that we want in public positions.'[18]

And then the candidate took to the stage.

2. The Alderman

'I often think what a great country ours would be if
we could but get rid of the blighting influences of
English misrule.'
Alderman Tom Kelly, 1911[1]

On 16 January 1911, Alfred Byrne was elected to Dublin City
Council. He was twenty-eight years old. At that time, local
government was weak in Ireland. In theory, a member of the
council was a powerful advocate for the public interest. In
practice, a member might attend a meeting, give a widely
ignored speech, gossip with rivals, pester a Corporation official, write to the papers, go to a funeral, spread good news
and stand himself on a cardboard box at the bottom of
Grafton Street. That was about it. This is not to say the job
was dull. There was always correspondence to attend to,
much of it heartbreaking.

The living conditions of many Dubliners were deplorable,
and the problem was acute in the centre of the city. Alfie and
Cissie had a flat above the Verdon bar on Talbot Street. Two
of Byrne's younger siblings, George and Edward, lived with
them, along with two servants; and later that year, Cissie
would give birth to a son, Tom. It was, by the standards of
the north inner city, still a small household. Others were not
so lucky: Byrne met the poor of Dublin on the streets every
morning. As a chatterbox and a good listener, *plámás* came

naturally to him. He was always and forever the man who promised to solve the problem, whatever it might be.

A political workhorse, Byrne joined seven committees in the Corporation – dealing with water, sanitation, housing and public health – as well as the Dublin Port and Docks Board and the Poor Law Board. And because the pub still demanded some of his attention, he was seldom at home. Cissie endured his long work hours and the fact that he couldn't go anywhere without being badgered for assistance. Patrick Byrne – at the time of writing, their only surviving child – remembers his father coming home for supper, 'and there would be notes in the margin of his newspapers, because people would stop him in the street to consult him about their problems. And after he had his evening meal he would transfer the notes from the papers into his big day book.' Hard-luck stories were radically condensed:

> Four foot from window.
> 8 Jones Lane Place.
> TB.[2]

Byrne became a father for the second time when Cissie gave birth to Alfred Junior at home on 12 June 1913. But his attention was soon diverted from domestic duties. James Larkin's Irish Transport and General Workers' Union (ITGWU) had developed a policy of sympathy strikes in support of other labour disputes. Seeking to crush Larkin and the ITGWU, four hundred employers, led by William Martin Murphy, imposed a full-scale lockout.

On 31 August, as strikers were gathered on O'Connell Street to listen to Larkin speak, police injured hundreds of Dubliners in baton charges. Three people died as a result of injuries received that day. Life for the poor, which had been difficult enough, now became unbearable, with many relying solely on handouts of bread and food parcels to stay alive.

Within a few weeks, some fifteen thousand union workers had been locked out, and many more non-union workers laid off. Byrne demanded that the Corporation's coal stores at the Pigeon House power station be used to provide fuel to the public at cost price. And while Dublin was at a standstill, he fought for the forty workers fired from the Port and Docks Board for refusing to unload reels of newsprint bound for William Martin Murphy's *Irish Independent*.[3] By February 1914, the dispirited strikers had effectively been starved back to work. The ITGWU attempted to get sacked workers rehired, and Byrne appealed on their behalf – unsuccessfully.

Like most Dubliners at that time, Byrne was outwardly religious. A regular at the short-twelve Mass in the Pro-Cathedral, he sat in the front pew on the Gospel side of the nave. (Patrick Byrne remembers that his father was 'a conforming Roman Catholic, but you couldn't say he was extremely religious'.) The Lockout provides an early example of his attachment to certain strands of Catholic thinking. When it was proposed that starving children of striking workers could be sent to families in England to escape extreme poverty, the Church protested vigorously, fearing that Protestant minders of the children might attempt to convert them. Byrne took part in protests against the removal of the children. 'He was doing what he did best,' says the historian Padraig Yeates. 'Following the mob to pick up a few votes.'[4]

The man who precipitated the Lockout, 'Big Jim' Larkin, was born in Liverpool to Irish parents. Robert Kee said of Larkin, 'His one concern, manically displayed through a powerful ego, was to organise effectively for their own welfare the wretched urban working classes of Ireland.' Another historian, F. S. L. Lyons, concluded, 'Like many great demagogues who thrive on the plaudits of the crowd, Larkin was at best an erratic administrator, quick-tempered, high-handed and temperamentally unsuited to the day-to-day manipulation of men.'[5]

Jim Larkin and Alfie Byrne both regarded themselves as champions of the poor, and over the decades to come they would often canvass for the same vote. During the local election campaign of 1914, stones were thrown at Byrne during public meetings. In the first incident, they narrowly missed their target. After the second incident, the *Irish Independent* reported, 'Stones were thrown, amidst cheers for [Jim] Larkin, and Mr Byrne, who was addressing the crowd from a brake, was struck on the forehead, receiving an ugly wound. He was assisted in a weak condition into the United Irish League rooms, where he collapsed.'

During that same campaign, Larkin called Byrne's pub, the Verdon, a 'sink of political and other corruption'.[6] Alcohol had long been used to canvass votes, making pubs central locations in the run-up to polling day.[7] In this case, Larkin said his Labour Party was defeated by an exotic alliance of 'slum landlords, scabs, prostitutes' bullies . . . Hibs, Orangemen, Temperance humbugs and porter sharks . . . the shopkeeper . . . the brothel keeper, the white slave trafficker . . . the parson, and many others, who had united to defeat labour'.[8] Larkin, who was a teetotaller, alleged that the Verdon was the headquarters for this conspiracy.

I would suggest to those who pretend to look after the morals and uplifting of the people to pass the Verdon Bar, Talbot Street today . . . why not all of you join your worthy alderman in the debauch which is now proceeding night and day? . . . Why not burn Larkin with prayer and incense, but don't forget the refreshing and stimulating porter which is the best friend the sweater, the slum landlord, and the politician can call upon.[9]

Larkin's attack on 'Alf Bung' made no difference to Dubliners, who knew Byrne as a semi-constant presence on the streets of his beloved north inner city. Canvassing came naturally to him. It was automatic and unthinking, like the 'B' in Byrne that brought him to the top of the ballot. He remembered what it was like to go to sleep on an empty stomach. And like any good barman, he knew how to make strangers feel special, so when he was writing your name on the edge of a newspaper, together with a summary of your plight, it was possible to imagine that something might be done about it.

The councillor who topped the poll in each ward was given the honorific title of Alderman; Byrne held that title for the next ten years. Larkin left for the United States that year, and in what became a nine-year absence the labour movement struggled to assert itself, partly because its base had been usurped by radical nationalism. That was the fashion. When Douglas Hyde resigned as President of the Gaelic League, he decried its politicization. Hyde's replacement was a Sinn Féin member of Dublin City Council called Seán T. O'Kelly.

In the summer of 1914, events on the continent ushered the United Kingdom into a war that would claim the lives of 723,000 British and Irish men and women.[10] In the background, the Home Rule Bill was, in the words of Thomas Bartlett, 'proceeding bumpily on its way to the statute books'.[11] All going well, Ireland would soon have its own parliament. The bill became law in September 1914, but was suspended until the end of the war. Crucially, it was agreed that six counties of Ulster were at least temporarily exempted from the Home Rule settlement.

The Ulster Volunteer Force, founded by unionists in January 1913, had acquired twenty-five thousand rifles, thus becoming the best armed force in the United Kingdom, apart from the British army itself. The Irish Volunteers, formed in response by nationalists, brought ashore a cache of out-of-date weapons in broad daylight at Howth in July 1914. Michael Laffan has written that W. T. Cosgrave, who was then a Sinn Féin member of Dublin City Council, loaded 'so many rifles into a taxi that he had difficulty in keeping the door closed'.[12] On their way back to Dublin, the Volunteers were intercepted at Bachelor's Walk by British soldiers; four people were killed. While Byrne was not involved with the gun-running, he was 'before the firing line on Sunday and helped the wounded', according to a photographic caption in the *Irish Independent*.[13]

As the old world came to an end, Byrne was plotting new ways to make money. On 28 August 1914, he incorporated a company in the name of the George's Street Picture Palace – thus following the example of James Joyce, who had set up Dublin's first cinema. Byrne was one of seven directors of the company, which raised £10,400 to build a cinema on the corner of South Great George's Street and Upper Stephen Street.[14] But after much deliberation the directors of the company decided not to proceed with their plan.

In October 1914, Byrne announced his intention to run for the post of Lord Mayor of Dublin. The mayor was chosen by the members of the City Council via the rather arcane procedural methods employed by the council in its daily business – motions, amendments, etc. In the early stages of the contest, Byrne withdrew in deference to a more senior colleague, Alderman John Clancy. However, when the sickly Clancy withdrew his nomination, Byrne resumed his bid, claiming that many members of the council had persuaded him to run. Then Clancy changed his mind again, and he was duly elected as Lord Mayor. In yet another twist, Clancy was never formally invested. On the way home from City Hall, he was caught in a rainstorm, took to his bed and promptly died of pneumonia. Another member ended up taking the position, thwarting Byrne's ambition once more.

The decision to run for mayor was a key moment in the self-creation of Alfie Byrne. It spoke to his energy and his burgeoning self-regard, and while he may never have had much chance of succeeding, Byrne had at least shown pluck. It would soon take him all the way to Westminster.

3. Mr Byrne Goes to London

'The future is veiled in mystery, but the doubts and
trepidations which for years past have so strenuously
assailed the conscientious student of contemporary
Irish history are rapidly disappearing and many of
them have already been relegated to the limbo of
forgetfulness. In the face of a common and terrible
danger, the country has been united as never before.'

Irish Times, 1 January 1916

As a result of the Great War, the British parliament of
1911 extended its lifetime twice before the general election of
1918. But there were several by-elections, including one in
the Harbour Division of Dublin, following the death of the
sitting MP, William Abraham of the Irish Party. The constituency was unusual in that it straddled both sides of the
River Liffey. On 7 September 1915, Alderman Alfred Byrne
announced that he would run for the seat.[1] This decision,
which was apparently the result of an after-hours chat with
two journalists in the Verdon bar, reflected the young man's
ambition, but also his personal circumstances.[2]

Byrne would later claim that the Verdon had been losing
money, and that he needed to sell the pub to pay for his campaign expenses. This may have been an exaggeration, but his
drive was real enough. After making the decision to sell the
pub, he threw himself at Dublin in the hope that the voters

would send him off to a well-paid job in the House of Commons.

The four-week election campaign was a rancorous affair. There were three nationalist candidates in the fray, and Byrne was seen as the outsider.[3] The fact that he was no longer a publican counted for nothing in the minds of his critics. W. R. Wigham, Secretary of the Irish Association for the Prevention of Intemperance, wrote an indignant letter to the *Irish Times*:

Dear Sir,

Will you allow me, for the guidance of voters interested in temperance, to state the following facts?

(1) The O'Mahony is a total abstainer, and for years has sub-scribed to this Association.

(2) Alderman J. J. Farrell entered the Corporation through the support of the temperance party, but his subsequent action has not justified that support.

(3) Alderman Alfred Byrne is a publican.

Yours, etc.[4]

The O'Mahony may have been sober, but he was a rum sort. Known variously as Pierce Charles De Lacy O'Mahony, The O'Mahony and The O'Mahony of Kerry, he would later become famous – according to that great repository of folk wisdom, Wikipedia – for having 'three names, two wives and three faiths, and for being honoured by the kings of two opposing countries in World War One'. While he was not of the working class himself, he claimed to have 'a deep interest in their welfare'. None of this endeared him to the people of East Wall:

The O'Mahony, on coming forward to address the meeting, was received with mingled cheering and booing. A section of the crowd was evidently hostile to the candidate, and never ceased its interruptions throughout his speech. He began by stating that in offering himself as a candidate at the election – (A Voice: 'And you are going to win, too' – cheers, and laughter) – his claim was that he had followed Charles Stewart Parnell faithfully to the end. It was a sad day when death deprived Ireland of her great leader. [The O'Mahony] had followed in the principles which he learned from Parnell down to the present day. (A Voice: – 'To your own profit.')[5]

Byrne was lucky that there was no Labour candidate in the race: James Connolly refused the nomination, and with the Labour movement still in disarray after the failure of the Lockout, no agreed candidate could be found. This enabled Byrne to cast himself as the voice of working-class Dublin, opposing conscription and penal wartime taxes, and generally sniping at the government.

On the morning of Saturday, 2 October 1915, when the ballot boxes were opened, it emerged that John J. Farrell had 617 votes to The O'Mahony's 913. Neither man had done nearly enough to secure the seat. With a total of 2,298 votes, the young Home Ruler from Seville Place was the new Member of Parliament for the Harbour Division of Dublin. Selling the pub had been a gamble, but it had paid off: suddenly, he could expect a spectacular salary of £400 a year. (At that time, a qualified engineer might make about £100.) Furthermore, Alfred Byrne MP would now represent the people of Dublin and the Irish Parliamentary Party in the Palace of Westminster.

A legend grew around Byrne's maiden speech in the House of Commons. On the same evening that he was elected in

Dublin, he was said to have taken the night boat to England, 'arrived in London at 8 a.m., hurried to the House of Commons, found that an all-night sitting had taken place and that the debate still went on, rose, caught the Speaker's eye, and made a speech which awakened a fair proportion of the somnolent legislators, and sat down a fully fledged Parliamentarian'.[6] This colourful tale may owe something to the example of John Redmond, who took his seat, made his maiden speech and was thrown out of the House, all within a few hours.[7] In fact, the new Member of Parliament for the Harbour Division of Dublin made his first contribution on 13 October 1915, twelve days after the election. After denouncing a claim that profits on the sale of alcohol had gone up, Byrne told the House of Commons:

> I, for one, would not have been in this House if it were not for the action of the House in imposing taxes on the licensing trade that it was unable to pay. I had to give up my licensing business only a month ago, as I was not able to find sufficient profit in it to pay outgoings. If I were able to continue in that trade in the City of Dublin I would be back there instead of being in the house now.[8]

Byrne soon fell for the rituals and pageantry of Westminster: the morning suits, the top hats, the esoteric rituals and the lavish surroundings. But he also took his duties as a backbencher seriously. Directing many of his questions to the Home Secretary or the Chief Secretary for Ireland, he spoke about factories in Ireland, army pensions and proposed increases to the cost of tea and sugar. 'I ask the Chancellor of the Exchequer seriously to consider the advisability of taking off the increase on tea and sugar, so giving the poor an opportunity of living.' He also demanded more factories in Ireland and 'better wages for Irish workers engaged in the making of munitions'.[9]

Byrne repeatedly warned the government that it would be foolish to introduce conscription in Ireland. In the absence of conscription, he argued, Ireland was a fruitful nursery for the British army: 'It has provided both soldiers and money, and, unless they wish to create serious trouble, the Government will under no circumstances attempt to introduce compulsion into Ireland.'

Byrne's voice was squeaky and easily assumed an indignant tone. Just five feet six inches tall, he was inclined to ramble, and his representations on behalf of impoverished constituents sometimes seemed at odds with his dapper appearance. In London he was, at least, surrounded by venerable duffers. At thirty-three, Byrne was one of the youngest MPs in the Irish Party. The oldest, Samuel Young, was ninety-four.

The mother of parliaments was a place where tradition meant a great deal, but not so much as verbal dexterity. (Disraeli: 'Mr Speaker, I withdraw my statement that half the Cabinet are asses. Half the Cabinet are not asses.') Loquacious rather than eloquent, Byrne could not tell the time without making a speech, and was fortunate to live in an age when politicians were not subject to regular scrutiny on television. He was a wordy opponent, then, but he was also dogged. When he warned that conscription in Ireland 'will be resisted by drilled and armed forces', the Prime Minister replied that he 'very much deprecated the threat contained in the last paragraph'. Although Byrne had only just arrived in London, the scrappy Dubliner was not afraid to goad the man who ruled over a quarter of the planet.

The political winds would soon shift, with the Liberals

blamed for dragging Britain into a protracted and extraordinarily bloody war and John Redmond's support for that war
proving divisive in Ireland. At a meeting of Dublin Corporation on 6 March 1916, Byrne joined with the leader of the
Sinn Féin group, W. T. Cosgrave, to propose a motion condemning the increasing tax burden in Ireland.[10] Anti-war
sentiment helped to build support for Cosgrave and his fellow republicans; the 'legion of the excluded' that would
declare war on the British empire at Easter 1916 included
Fenians, socialists, Gaelic Leaguers, politicized women and
the young. One of the things that united them was impa-
tience with the old Irish Party. Talking had secured nothing.

As a piece of street theatre, the Easter Rising was spectacular. (Over at Liberty Hall, passers-by asked Constance
Markievicz if she was rehearsing a play for children.) As an
act of revolution, it was hopeless. German help never arrived;
the head of the Irish Volunteers tried to call the whole thing
off; the rebels didn't have enough food and water; there was
no supply system in place; and the buildings seized by the
rebels were chosen more for dramatic effect than military
strategy. When asked about the rebels' chances, James Connolly is said to have replied: 'None whatever.'

Byrne was in Dublin during the Rising. He opposed it
and, unlike many Dubliners, never pretended otherwise.
(*Dublin Opinion* once joked that an extension should be added
to the General Post Office to accommodate everyone who
was out in 1916.) When the rebellion started, Byrne was
recruited as an officer of the peace by Francis Sheehy Skeffington, a pacifist who had previously been jailed for
campaigning against recruitment to the British army.[11] They
took to the streets in white armbands, urging Dubliners not

to loot shops. Standing near the Nelson Pillar, 'too scared to stay, too curious to go', Byrne saw a group of Lancers on horseback approaching the GPO. Many years later, he provided this account of what happened next:

> It was a sight to make your blood tingle . . . their horses capering and the morning sun catching the gleam of their long poles . . . Just as lancers passed the Nelson Pillar, a volley rang out above their heads, a warning from the post office. The sight of what happened then, I will never forget. A single lancer detached himself and came back down the street at a walk, and when he came to the Pillar there was a single shot. The lancer still walked his horse. Another shot, and still the horseman held his pace. But the third shot tumbled him off the beast, so that his foot caught in the stirrup and carried him bumping along with his head striking the cobbles as the animal lunged. It was a terrifying sight . . . Two young girls ran out from Henry Street . . . and while one snatched the bridle of the lunging steed, the other unloosed the lancer's foot, so that his body fell and lay against the curbing. [It was] a gallant act of mercy by lasses little more than school children.[12]

When the tricolour was raised on the roof of the GPO, Byrne was across the road, trying to stop people from looting. There are accounts of girls in fur coats, but the most popular targets were sweet shops, including Noblett's, which was famous for its extravagant window displays. They presented the poor with an appetizing target in the absence of authority.[13] At least one person was killed that week for the want of a jelly baby. This hagiographical account was published in the *Church of Ireland Gazette* in 1937:

Byrne, wearing the white armlet of the little corps, made manful endeavour with the others to stem the tide of fierce covetousness which swept through big sections of the city's non-combatants when the big stores stood temptingly unguarded in the midst of rebellion, and which rose eventually to swamp the whole central shopping quarters of Dublin. During Monday and Tuesday, Byrne and his comrades, parading Sackville-street, did good work in protecting the shops. Only on Wednesday did Byrne retire from a hopeless task, as street warfare crackled more heavily just before it burst into the consuming flame that burnt out the city's heart.

On the following day, however,

he was out again in a gallant sally through the bullet-swept streets to bring bread to half-starving neighbours. All trading had stopped, householders were eking out their food supplies, many working class families in the immediate area were in desperate plight. Alfie used his influence as MP to obtain a permit to bring a borrowed bread-van [from] a well-known bakery. In great risk of the bullets of both sides, Alfie and two volunteer helpers made their way cautiously up Earl Street, many buildings of which were then ablaze. They found the bakery stables burned and almost a dozen dead horses lying there. The van was loaded up, however, with its sorely needed bread.

After 'further perilous journeying', the bread was delivered to two convents; one of them, St Laurence O'Toole's, was beside Byrne's birthplace on Seville Place. By the time Byrne and the van driver, Joe Kennedy, were making their way home, it was after curfew: 'A military patrol with fixed bayonets seized them suddenly at Newcomen Bridge, put them into an empty house, and rigorously interrogated them ... After a thoroughly anxious hour, however, their bona-fides were accepted. Alfie and Joe were permitted to return home – with an official caution.'[14]

Francis Sheehy Skeffington was not so lucky. On the Tuesday of Easter Week, while walking home to Rathmines, Sheehy Skeffington was followed by a crowd of hecklers, and arrested by soldiers. Captain J. C. Bowen-Colthurst used him as a human shield while raiding a tobacconist's shop. Later, along with two other men, Sheehy Skeffington was shot by a firing squad summarily convened by Bowen-Colthurst.

By the time the rebels surrendered on 29 April, 485 people – including forty children – were dead, the majority of them civilians. Three thousand more were wounded. Most of the civilian casualties were men, women and children from the centre of the city: Byrne's people. It is true that some Dubliners jeered at the rebels as they were led through the streets, but by the time the executions began, hostility had given way to admiration, and then to outrage at the British authorities for covering up the killing of Sheehy Skeffington and the others.

On 3 May, Patrick Pearse was executed by firing squad. His younger brother Willie perished in the same fashion the following day. Byrne told the House of Commons the execution of the Pearse brothers 'is such a crime as will be remembered for the next hundred years as one of the blackest crimes ever committed by the English Government against Ireland. The shooting of Pearse, Junior, because he was a brother of Pearse, Senior, is a thing which can never be excused.' As usual, he was reflecting public opinion on the streets of Dublin.

Some 1,800 rebels were sent to Frongoch in Wales, which had previously served as a makeshift prison for captured German soldiers. In the summer of 1916, Byrne visited Frongoch, Knutsford and several other places of detention. Michael Collins wrote to thank him: 'We appreciate your humanitarian efforts and all you have done for the boys here.'[15] But others were less welcoming. A member of the ITGWU and the Irish Citizen Army, Frank Robbins, berated his fellow prisoners for talking to Byrne: 'You ought to be ashamed of yourselves, allowing this man to fool you. Have you forgotten why you are here?'[16]

An essentially conservative figure, Byrne did not approve of violent revolution. He always described himself as a 'constitutional' and, after independence was secured in 1922, he called for better relations with Britain. But as soon as the Rising was over, Byrne argued that the rebels should be treated not as traitors to the Crown but as political prisoners. He did all that he could to improve their situation, aware – unlike many in his party – that a profound political shift had occurred. It is possible to see Byrne's actions in Easter Week and its aftermath as those of a man who was simply trying to save his own career. That is to ignore the depth of his compassion.

Helena Molony, a member of Inghinidhe na hÉireann, was involved in the raid on Dublin Castle. Captured, Molony spent most of Easter Week in Kilmainham Gaol, attempting to dig her way out with a spoon, before being imprisoned in England.[17] In 1952, Molony wrote a letter to Byrne in which she remembered his visits 'to us women prisoners in the early dark days of 1916 – before the swing of opinion in Ireland made our movement prove popular'.[18] On one occasion, Byrne managed to take some of the female prisoners out to tea. They were accompanied by two uniformed wardresses, and in her letter Molony saluted 'the moral courage it took to lead such a party into a fashionable restaurant in the City of London on a summer afternoon. It took a noble-hearted gentleman and a chivalrous knight to do such a thing and we all appreciated it, enhanced – as it was – by the fact that we all belonged to a different and hostile political party.'[19] In parliament, Byrne demanded to know when 'the Irish lady prisoners will ever have an opportunity of receiving what you boast of as British justice, or will they ever get any justice?'

When Byrne visited Countess Markievicz in Aylesbury Prison, she was not in her cell. According to Markievicz's biographer Anne Marreco, 'When he tracked her down finally he found her with her pail and brush, and she asked him gaily if he had guessed that she would know how to scrub.' After the visit, Byrne asked the Chief Secretary if he knew that she had 'to mix with the lowest criminals in the land?' When was he going to 'improve the prison food and her general surroundings'? Some time later, the countess had a note to Byrne smuggled out from prison: 'I wanted to tell you how glad I was to hear of all the great work you are doing – we may meet again in happier days.'[20] When she was temporarily released, Byrne took her for tea on the terrace of the House of Commons. The meeting was apparently interrupted by Irish members of the House of Lords, because etiquette required them to greet their peer the Countess.[21] In her witness statement to the Bureau of Military History, Marie Perolz recalled being treated by Byrne to 'a grand tea, including strawberries and cream, at a Lyons' shop'.

In the summer of 1916, attention turned away from Ireland as the political establishment struggled to comprehend the scale of the losses incurred at the Battle of the Somme – twenty thousand British soldiers were killed on the first day alone. (Charles Findlater, Byrne's first employer, was killed during the last British attack of the battle.) But the MP from Dublin kept talking about the rebels: 'Since I came to this House I have seen very little of that boasted English chivalry. I desire to refer to the prisoners in gaol, who have been kept there for the last three months without trial . . . Are the Government afraid to give these men a fair trial in a Civil Court?' In one prison, he said, 'black and sour' bread was given out to eat, the place was infested with rats, and 'thirty or forty [prisoners] were thrown into one room, 12ft. by 14 ft. square. They [have] to eat, drink, and sleep in that room with a leaking dustbin in the room as the only lavatory accommodation.' Many years later, Joseph V. Lawless recalled one of Byrne's prison sorties:

> Mr Byrne was not held as other visitors were in the separate visitors' yard, but was conducted by a pompous staff sergeant into the prisoners' exercise yard where we were all at play. No one took much notice at first of the top-hatted figure until the sergeant announced in a loud voice 'Mr Alfred Byrne, MP.' Then he was recognised and was greeted by a chorus of yells from bearded faces – 'Ah, the hard Alfie', 'Up Dublin' and the like. I think the sergeant was slightly shocked by such wanton familiarity as the crowd gathered around Alfie and received his bountiful distribution of packets of Woodbines, the while they plied him with questions.[22]

Back in Dublin, a majority of the City Council backed Byrne's demand for 'the release of our fellow countrymen and women interned in English prisons, without trial, and an Amnesty for those who have been sentenced to terms of imprisonment'. Byrne also lobbied on behalf of imprisoned members of the council, such as W. T. Cosgrave, and raised the case of a political rival in parliament. 'Is [the Chief Secretary] aware that the refusal to remove hard labour disqualifies Councillor [Patrick] Mahon from attending his public duties, and that such disqualification is resented by Mr Mahon's constituents?'

When Roger Casement – an Irishman knighted for his services to the British empire, before his decision to support the Rising – was tried for treason in the summer of 1916, Byrne lobbied for his release. But extracts of Casement's diaries (containing what R. F. Foster has called 'an extraordinarily full record of his compulsive sexual adventures') were circulated to influential figures in British society, doing immeasurable damage to his reputation.[23]

At Casement's trial, Byrne would have seen another Irishman, John Lavery, painting a large picture of the scene. An orphan from Belfast, Lavery made a name for himself as a painter to the stars, and his decision to depict Casement sympathetically was, in the words of Barbara Dawson, 'an extremely brave undertaking for an artist whose livelihood was derived primarily from those opposed to political change'.[24] Lavery's picture was panned in the British press. Like Byrne and others, he may have thought that the Casement diaries were fake. Byrne made appeals on behalf of Casement to the Prime Minister and his entire Cabinet. Then he tried to raise the matter in the House of Commons. The *Sunday Chronicle* printed this account of what happened next:

The Speaker informed [Byrne] that 'questions affecting advice tendered to His Majesty on matters of reprieve were not allowed in the House.' There was no more to do; he would be ruled instantly out of order if he referred to Casement. Careful, determined officialdom had ensured that he should not enter the House to create any trouble about Casement. He had been warned. It was clear too, that the mind of the Government was against Casement. The memorials, the suggestions, all the hopes and beliefs and appeals were in vain. The little junior MP walked on again to his seat, slowly, sadly, as three o'clock chimed ponderously from Big Ben.[25]

Roger Casement was executed for treason on 3 August 1916. By that stage, public opinon in Dublin had deserted the Irish Party. Seventeen years later, Con O'Leary wrote: '[Byrne] stood out from his colleagues in interpreting the new spirit that was sweeping over the Nationalist Ireland. He was the first to warn Mr Redmond . . . that if a general election occurred half the members of the party would lose their seats to Sinn Féin.'[26]

Byrne continued to badger the government with requests on behalf of the Irish rebels. He demanded additional underclothing, books and papers, and wanted to know why a prisoner was given a second-hand copy of the Bible 'found on a book-hawker's barrow in London'. He ended one speech with a withering rebuke to the government of the mightiest empire the world had ever known:

> Six months have now virtually passed since the rebellion in Ireland, and I have been endeavouring to obtain some humane and proper treatment for the Irish prisoners . . . The mockery and the insincerity of the whole thing as applied to Ireland is very painfully seen in the treatment of the Irish prisoners at Frongoch. There is no humanity, no

protection for the Irish ... Does the Right Hon. Gentleman think that is the right way to treat those prisoners?
They fought for what they believed to be the best interests
of their country. Is it not time that he should release them?

In July 1917, Byrne's father, Tom, died at home on the North
Strand Road. The *Freeman's Journal* reported that the funeral
cortege 'was representative of every shade of opinion in Dublin'.[27] Two months later, the junior member for the Harbour
Division was the only representative of the Irish Party at the
funeral of Thomas Ashe, a veteran of the Rising who died in
prison after being force-fed on the sixth day of a hunger strike.
Ashe's death at the age of thirty-two convulsed nationalist Ireland, leading to another surge in support for Sinn Féin.

John Redmond died the following spring, and in the general election of December 1918 the Home Rule movement
was effectively buried by the electorate.[28] The Irish Party
went into the contest with sixty-eight seats and came out
with just six. It was one of the worst electoral thrashings in
modern European history. And like so many of his colleagues, Byrne lost his seat to a Sinn Féin candidate:

Philip Shanahan: 7,708 (58.87%)
Alfred Byrne: 5,386 (41.13%)

It was a galling defeat for an ambitious young politician
who had seen the danger and done his utmost to champion
the cause of imprisoned republicans. But Byrne remained
friendly with his opponent, the publican Phil Shanahan, and
came to his defence long after his death. In 1937, a rival
lamented the time when publican-politicians 'thought more
of their profits than of Kathleen ni Houlihan'. Byrne stood

up for his breed: 'In the old days when our people had no lands or votes, the licensed vintners were behind Parnell, who got the people both the land and the vote which brought about the freedom we possess.' Claiming that publicans were the backbone of the national movement, he cited Shanahan, whose profits were used 'to buy guns for the men who fought for this country, and to whom the State owed at least £20,000 for money spent to help the country'.[29]

Although there must have been an element of political calculation in his work on behalf of republican prisoners, Byrne spent the rest of his life fighting for veterans of the revolution. As late as 1952, at the age of seventy-two, he asked the Dublin Board of Assistance to give an IRA pension to a woman in Crumlin. Two government ministers had already failed to meet his demand. 'I have a personal knowledge of her activities in the IRA Movement – in 1916 she was actively engaged in Dublin, Cork and Limerick,' he wrote. 'I know if it lies in your power to make the old lady's days happy, you will do so.'[30]

4. Free State Politician

Alfie Byrne never joined another political party after the Sinn Féin landslide of December 1918. Some of his colleagues in the Irish Party would decide to withdraw from political life, but Byrne was still young, he was still an alderman, privy to the chit-chat of revolution in City Hall, and there were still many Dubliners who regarded him as a champion – or, as an opponent called him, 'a tin god'.[1] By this point, he was also a father of three. Cissie would give birth to ten children, of whom eight survived to adulthood. The second son, Tom, was learning to walk when the IRA launched a guerrilla war against the British. For the second time in three years, Dublin became a battlefield.

In the local elections of January 1920, Byrne ran as an independent candidate. Proving that he was a formidable vote-getter in his own right, he secured 3,180 votes against a Sinn Féin candidate who got only 826.[2] Later that year, he made a pair of property investments. First, he bought two fine houses, 23 and 24 Dartmouth Square, for a total of £1,260. (He would move his family into 23 and sell 24.) Then, in partnership with five other men, he bought several hundred acres of land at Kilmartin, Castleknock.[3] The solicitor who represented Byrne in both deals was Henry Lemass, a cousin of the young revolutionary Seán Lemass. (Henry Lemass worked for Hanna Sheehy Skeffington when she demanded justice after the murder of her husband, Francis, in 1916. It is possible that Byrne made the introduction. The following year, Byrne helped Sheehy Skeffington to secure equal pay for women in Dublin Corporation.)

Dublin was the scene of numerous violent skirmishes during the War of Independence. Many years later, a man called Austin P. Kelly would write to Byrne about an incident near Newcomen Bridge, which crosses the Royal Canal – the same bridge where Byrne had been interrogated by British soldiers during the Easter Rising. On this occasion, republican forces ambushed four soldiers on the bridge, as Kelly recalled:

> You had just left your home, and had reached the foot of Newcomen Bridge ... suddenly there was an awful commotion, I noticed a car had stopped down and some fellows standing up, blazing away in your direction [. . .]. I can vividly remember pulling you to the ground, somewhat roughly I am afraid. I was scared to death, but I like to think with a certain amount of pride, if you will forgive me for being so presumptuous, that I share in a very small way, the honour of saving a very fine and gallant gentleman from what could have been a genuine loss to dear old Dublin, perhaps I should say the nation at large.[4]

Byrne wrote back to Kelly, recalling the moment 'when the lorry passed and I think it was a hand grenade which was thrown. We were all hussled into a shop at the corner of Newcomen Court and I was at the wrong end of a rifle! The man in possession was trembling with fear and so was I, because I was at the wrong end.'

In the autumn of 1921, following a truce, Éamon de Valera sent Arthur Griffith, Michael Collins and three other plenipotentiaries to London to negotiate a political settlement with the British. The resulting Anglo-Irish Treaty secured independence, but the new Irish Free State fell short of a republic: it would be a dominion of the British Commonwealth. Members of the nascent parliament would have to take an oath of allegiance, and the six counties of Northern Ireland could opt not to join the Irish Free State. A natural conservative and a strictly constitutional nationalist, Byrne supported the Anglo-Irish Treaty.

The Five Lamps, a crossroads on the northside of the city, was the dead centre of Byrne's world, and his favourite location for campaign speeches. (It was a hundred yards from his birthplace.) Running for a Dáil Éireann seat in the 1922 general election – the first in the Irish Free State – Byrne told the faithful that he was an Independent nationalist. It worked. He was elected as a TD for the Dublin Mid constituency in 1922, and again in 1923. After the first of these victories he told supporters, 'I cannot explain the enormous vote. My humble efforts in public life, I am afraid, have been greatly exaggerated.'[5] That combination of modesty and self-promotion was classic Dublin, but also classic Byrne. So, too, was a notice he published in the *Evening Herald*:

> To the men and women who voted for me I offer you my grateful appreciation for the high honour they have conferred by electing me to be one of their representatives for the district in which I, my father and my grandfather were born. Sympathy or thanks are useless to the many thousands of unemployed men and women now in the city; but to those in the ranks of that huge army who wrote to me, and whose letters remain unanswered, I assure that every possible effort of mine will be exerted to secure for them decent, remunerative employment and decent wages.[6]

In the House of Commons, Byrne had discovered that

power often wears a uniform. Now returned to Dublin, this short, undistinctive man in his early forties dressed for a role in a costume drama, or even a comedy by Oscar Wilde. ('A well-tied tie is the first serious step in life.') The top hat lent height, while a cane is always a useful symbol of authority. In person, he seemed excessively courteous, too, using manners as a weapon and flattery as its advance party. Costume and charm were essential assets in the seduction of Dublin.

With the onset of civil war, Dublin again became the scene of urban warfare. Many years later, a constituent reminded Byrne about the time 'when we were burned out of our homes in Findlater Place during the trouble of 1922. We would have been left homeless if it had not been for [your] persistent harrying of the Corporation at that time.'[7] Although he was firmly on the pro-Treaty side, Byrne demanded humane treatment for the republicans who had occupied the Four Courts, and he complained to the government about being denied access to the prisons.[8] (The following year, after Noel Lemass, who fought on the anti-Treaty side with his brother Seán, disappeared in broad daylight in a busy part of the city, Byrne expressed alarm in the Dáil 'surrounding the disappearance of Mr Noel Lemass, which took place on Tuesday, 3 July 1923, in broad daylight, in a much frequented thoroughfare of the city'. It was probably too late. The mutilated body of Noel Lemass would be found in October 1923, providing a gruesome coda to the Civil War.)

In September 1922, Byrne's former council colleague W. T. Cosgrave became President of the Executive Council, following the deaths of two of the chief architects of the Free State the previous month: Arthur Griffith had succumbed to heart failure, and ten days later, Michael Collins was killed in an ambush by anti-Treaty forces. Also in September, Byrne, too, found himself elevated to a position of consequence, when the Lord Mayor of Dublin, Laurence O'Neill, became ill: a temporary replacement was needed. To serve as Lord Mayor *locum tenens*, O'Neill chose Alderman Byrne, praising his 'tact and good nature'.[9] Both Cosgrave and Byrne were innately conservative politicians educated by the Christian Brothers in a poor part of Dublin. Both had worked in the pub business. Both were pious Catholics. They would remain friends for the next thirty years and, most of the time, Byrne would support Cosgrave's party in the Dáil.

With its gold chains and esoteric conventions, the post of Lord Mayor appealed to Byrne. An introduction to civic leadership that chimed with his experience in London, he liked the pageantry and the power, or at least the illusion of power. (Auberon Waugh: 'The urge to power is a personality disorder in its own right, like the urge to sexual congress with children or the taste for rubber underwear.') Byrne must have contemplated the prospect of securing the office in the normal fashion, rather than keeping the seat warm for someone else. But that possibility was about to disappear. Local government was among the casualties of the Civil War.

The historian Diarmaid Ferriter has written of the 'utter contempt that quickly developed at central government level for local democracy'.[10] Centralized control became a primary aim of the Free State government, and a corruption scandal was the pretext for a shake-up. It was alleged that certain councillors had committed misconduct 'in relation to the allocation of houses at the Corporation's Fairbrother's Field housing scheme'.[11] The outcome of the inquiry was the suspension of the corporation. For six years, three commissioners exercised the functions of the corporation. The sky did not fall in.

After the revolution, independence and a bitter Civil War, it was time for the prosaic reality of state-building. As the country's first head of government, Cosgrave was never accused of excessive dynamism, but he provided stability to a newly born and deeply divided state at a time when many European nations dispensed with democracy altogether. This was a significant achievement, particularly given the economic situation. In 1922, over thirty thousand Dubliners were out of work. By 1925, a quarter of all deaths in the city were of children under the age of five.[12]

After independence, the Dublin Metropolitan Police was disbanded, the Four Courts were rebuilt, the Monto – Dublin's red-light district – was shut down, a public telephone was installed on College Green, red post-boxes were painted green and street names were changed to honour patriotic heroes. But these were modest advances. None improved the lives of Dubliners in the way, for example, the arrival of the old-age pension had done under British rule. For many of Byrne's constituents, there was little to celebrate about life in the Irish Free State.

> I am in trouble and really don't know what to do. I buried my daughter aged fourteen years on Monday from the Hospice for the Dying. Complaint heart trouble [*sic*] and other complications. Her daddy died four years ago, I tried to keep the family together but owing [to] being ill now and again I happened to be elapsed out of burial insurance. Now I have no money to pay for the funeral expenses and I am wondering if you could help me in any way or advise me where to go. I am not in the habit of looking for charity but now I would be glad of anything that would help. I have four more children.[13]

Dáil Éireann sat in Leinster House, in a lecture hall

provided by the Royal Dublin Society. It was supposed to be a temporary home for the national parliament. Byrne urged Cosgrave to take over the old parliament house in College Green. But the new government was broke, or, as Cosgrave put it, 'I doubt very much whether the Old Parliament House would be found convenient for the needs of a modern parliament.'[14] One of Byrne's earliest contributions to Dáil Éireann was a request for speeches made in Irish to be translated into English, for the benefit of members who did not speak the native tongue.

Many successful people have two voices: public and familiar. Byrne had a pompous manner when making speeches, but offstage he used his voice and natural charm in a way that enchanted Dubliners of every class. In the first of two general elections in 1927, Byrne secured more votes than any other candidate in the country. To do so without the backing of a party machine was a remarkable feat of vote-getting.

1. Alfie Byrne	Dublin North	17,780
2. Kevin O'Higgins	Dublin County	15,918
3. William T. Cosgrave	Carlow-Kilkenny	13,272
4. Éamon de Valera	Clare	13,029
5. Richard Mulcahy	Dublin North	11,726

In trying to explain his success, a reporter wrote in the *Sunday Independent*:

You remember the dapper, doughty little man with the winning way and the business manner who made the wonderful maiden speech in the House of Commons in the Home Rule days? Well, that's he.

So this retiring, genial little Dublin man – 'Alfie' to all his friends – stands alone in Merrion Buildings. He is a party to himself. He has no organisation, no backing, no Big Noise to shout him along. During the campaign he made no speeches, made no promises and fielded no meetings . . . I think it was Fénelon who said: 'I love my country better than my family, but I love human nature better than my country.' 'Alfie' is like that.[15]

Like many other men who are synonymous with the northside of Dublin, Byrne made his home on the southside. The large Victorian house on Dartmouth Square in Ranelagh offered plenty of room for his growing family. Neighbours on the square included Frank Duff, founder of the Legion of Mary, and the actor Barry Fitzgerald. In 1927, a former neighbour told Byrne about his tyrannical landlady on Seville Place. 'My wife and children are daily subjected to insults from her . . . even the back garden is "out of bounds" to the children.'[16] But the right of kids to roam freely was also a problem on the southside. Byrne once printed a leaflet offering ten pounds to anyone with information on 'the intentions of the original designers as to the use of the Park surrounded by Houses known as Dartmouth Square'. Residents and their children were being deprived of 'the use of the Park as enjoyed by them for the past thirty years'. (The matter remained unresolved until 2012, when the City Council bought the square, ensuring public access in perpetuity.)

In the Dáil, Byrne's contributions veered between the declamatory and the whimsical, like Laurel *and* Hardy. He asked the Minister for Finance to 'take steps to prevent the importation of a lot of the rubbish now being sold in Dublin which is called wine'. In 1928, he said the government should regulate advertising in public places. (He once tried to ban advertising on Radio Éireann.) When the old-age pension was cut, Byrne denounced the decision, and he often railed against the border, 'the greatest crime against the peace and prosperity of Ireland'.[17]

A year and a half after his champion display of vote-getting, Byrne decided to step sideways. Elections to the Senate were held every three years at that time, unlinked to general elections; the next one was coming up in December 1928. After a long stretch in public life, Byrne said, he was exhausted. Serving in the Senate would be less gruelling, allowing more time for constituency work. That was, at any rate, the official explanation for his decision to resign from the Dáil:

> Mr Byrne told the Political Correspondent of the *Irish Independent* last night that the abolition of the Dublin Corporation and Guardians, as well as the unemployed problem, had placed so much additional work on his shoulders in attending to the needs of his constituents that he was considering whether he might not be compelled to retire from public life, after eighteen years' activity, because of the strain on his health. His friends, he says, desire him to remain a member of the Oireachtas and as the work in the Seanad is less strenuous than in the Dáil, he would have more time to devote to the demands being made on him outside the legislature.[18]

Byrne was duly elected a senator. Upon resigning his seat in the Dáil, it was taken by a candidate from Cumann na nGaedheal, as Cosgrave's party was now known. Patrick Byrne thinks that his father resigned his Dáil seat to create a place for Dr Tom O'Higgins, brother of the late justice minister, Kevin O'Higgins, who had been murdered by the IRA in 1927. There is no direct evidence to support this conjecture, although we do know that the political support of Cumann na nGaedheal would be crucial in the coming years. This may have been the first major test of his fidelity to the party.

In 1929, Senator Byrne was appointed as a trustee of the Royal Liver Friendly Society – a role previously held by one of his political mentors, J. P. Nannetti. The society had been set up 'to provide for the decent interment of deceased members'. In addition to providing Byrne with an income, the position was a useful way to garner votes. A journalist once asked Byrne to see if he could help him to get a house: 'I understand that your Association, the Liver National Health, by reason of its investments in Corporation stock for housing purposes has the right of nomination of tenants.'[19] Being a trustee of the Royal Liver was not demanding. Byrne had to sign insurance policies and other documents, and attend the society's annual conference, held in places such as Llandudno or Blackpool. Some years later, he was on Royal Liver business when he bumped into David Lloyd George in the bathroom of a hotel in Torquay. 'Aha!' said the former Prime Minister, 'the Honourable Member for the Harbour Division!'[20]

Dublin Corporation was restored in 1930, with a wider geographical reach that encompassed suburban districts south of the Grand Canal: Rathmines, Pembroke and Rathgar. From now on, a city manager with his own staff, and separate departments for finance, public health, streets and waterworks, would report directly to thirty-five elected members.

An independent review had concluded that the post of Lord Mayor should be abolished: it was anachronistic, a waste of money and synonymous with the *ancien régime*. But tradition won out. The 265th Lord Mayor of Dublin would be elected to chair meetings, officiate at events, welcome dignitaries and represent the city to the world.

Anticipating the advent of the new Corporation, the *Donegal News* observed:

> Byrne ... deputised for the Lord Mayor during a most troubled period, and the impartial way in which he conducted the business of the City Council won for him the praises of all sections of the community. The humblest citizen with the smallest grievance can place his or her case in his hands, and he has devoted much time and attention to the cause of the poor.[21]

In the autumn of 1930, Byrne once again found himself preparing for a City Council election. He placed an advertisement in the *Evening Herald*, warning voters that his old rival Jim Larkin – standing in the same district – 'claims to be the direct representative of Soviet Russia, and retains the Soviet Flag'. On polling day, Byrne was assaulted by supporters of Larkin outside a polling station. He collapsed, but recovered in time to address a meeting shortly after the incident. Later the same day, the *Cork Examiner* found him 'minding [a] baby in a pram while mother went to vote. Kindly man that he is, he would have done it even if aware that mother was hostile to him.'[22]

Byrne topped the poll, but Larkin was elected as well – as was his son, Jim Larkin Jr. Commenting on the results, the *Roscommon Herald* observed:

> [The old] Corporation was abolished for fear one Jim Larkin would get into it, and now, when it has been revived after a long period of incubation, it produces not one Jim Larkin but two. Dublin's Corporation has something in

common with Dublin Stout. The longer it was kept bottled up, the more gas it produced.[23]

Shortly after the election, when a reporter saw Alfie and Big Jim in conversation, he was struck by 'the friendliness between these old political opponents. They have been hammering at each other for nearly twenty years – and yet here they were exchanging handshakes and smiles and pleasantries just like brothers.'[24]

When the City Council met on 14 October 1930, the first item on the order of business was the election of the new Lord Mayor. Given the fractured make-up of the council, the winner would need support across multiple political factions. Laurence O'Neill and Seán T. O'Kelly TD were among the candidates. When O'Neill was eliminated in the first round of voting, he had the good grace to nominate his protégé in the second round. Byrne was in the race.

Now the speeches started: the solemn references to his good character; Westminster and Frongoch; his service to the poor of Dublin. Finally, after a fractious two-and-a-half-hour debate, each councillor was asked to choose a candidate in a show of hands. In the end, Alfie Byrne defeated Seán T. O'Kelly by twenty votes to thirteen.

Byrne won the mayoralty with the assistance of Cumann na nGaedheal. In return for their continued support, he would give his vote to them, and later to Fine Gael, in parliament. The Home Ruler from Seville Place had brokered a formidable deal; one that survived for many years.

Byrne's victory was widely celebrated, with the London *Evening Standard* touting the rags-to-riches story: 'He has risen from a seven shilling a week job in a bicycle shop at the foot of Dawson Street to the Mansion House at the top of the same street.' That journey of barely three hundred metres in thirty-six years was all the more extraordinary because it established a record that will surely never be broken.[25] Alfie Byrne had just become the first and only man in history to serve as councillor, alderman, MP, TD, senator and Lord Mayor of Dublin.

5. The Pied Piper of Dawson Street

What [Byrne] stands for it is difficult to say;
everybody agrees that he is a 'decent sort', and all
classes give him their votes. Generally he supports
the Government; but he is not really much concerned
with party politics . . . In debate he is sometimes
merely fatuous, but he will nearly wear the shoes off
his feet in worrying Government departments on
behalf of any poor man whom he considers a
deserving case – and he exercises a wondrous charity
in his interpretation of the word 'deserving'.

Belfast Newsletter, 18 October 1930

The Mansion House was built by Joshua Dawson, one of the leading property developers in eighteenth-century Dublin. He sold the grand residence to Dublin Corporation for £3,500, a price that included tapestries, silk curtains, gilt leather hangings and four pairs of scarlet calamanco window curtains. The Corporation bought the house, contents and gardens free of all rent – except, that is, for an annual premium of one loaf of double refined sugar of six pounds weight – and established it as the official home of the Lord Mayor of Dublin.

In October 1930, the new Lord Mayor plotted his journey from Dartmouth Square to Dawson Street, ordering repairs and renovations that cost £5,000. The work did not take place until the following summer, and the showpiece home would not be fully habitable until the Eucharistic Congress of 1932, when it was used as accommodation for visiting clergy. In the meantime, Senator Byrne put his own house on the market – 'a very arrogant thing to do!', in the words of his son Patrick – and requisitioned a small section of the Mansion House, where he hung paintings by George Romney, Sir Joshua Reynolds and 'one of the best portraits of Queen Victoria in her younger days'.[1]

The new Lord Mayor soon needed help to cope with the volume of correspondence. The Corporation supplied only a secretary and a steward, so Byrne hired 'an additional secretary, a chauffeur, and three maids who were paid from his private pocket'.[2] In City Hall, Jim Larkin complained when it was revealed that the annual salary for the Lord Mayor would rise from £1,600 to £2,500.[3] Larkin demanded that Byrne's salary be cut to £2,000, but it was ruled that the figure was specified in a contract between Dublin Corporation and the Lord Mayor, and could not be altered. Byrne would be the highest-paid politician in the country, a measure of his negotiating skills and the prestige attached to the job. In some mysterious way, the publicity surrounding his salary made him more magnetic, as if the people of Dublin felt his riches might rub off on them.

Byrne quickly developed a reputation as an expert on bread and circuses. One of his first major decisions was to entertain school children at tea parties in the Mansion House. Over two thousand children enjoyed cocoa and cake at the first Christmas feast, everyone was presented with a personalized box of Urney chocolates at the end, and there were even special trams to take the young guests home. Many Dubliners had what one later correspondent called 'the privilege of shaking hands with you at the entrance to the Round Room of the Mansion House',[4] and the party played well in the press. The *Evening Mail* congratulated Byrne for resurrecting 'some of the benevolent grace and charm of human existence in the long-neglected halls of the Mansion House' and told readers that the Lord Mayor was bringing 'at least one day of real joy to the hearts of the little ones, too many of whom are doomed to live the best part of their lives in squalid and unhealthy surroundings'. The same article referenced Byrne's financial situation in a way that would not have pleased Jim Larkin:

> No doubt, apart from his allowance of £2,500 a year as Lord Mayor, Senator Byrne is a comparatively wealthy man; but does not our experience in this cynical and selfish age go to show that others just as wealthy would take the position and save money on their salary and obligations without a thought for their social obligations?[5]

The lavish parties – and those column inches – demonstrate two of Byrne's skills as a politician. A seminal figure in the history of pester power, he used children to do his bidding in a way that would raise concerns today – urging them, for example, to canvass their parents at the kitchen table. At one election, kids stood outside the voting booths with photographs of Byrne around their necks. And for many years, a schoolyard chant included the words, 'Cheer up, Alfie Byrne is knocking at the door.' In the folklore of the city, the Children's Lord Mayor was the great provider of lollipops and sweets, games in parks and free school meals.

In Terence Dolan's *Dictionary of Hiberno-English*, the Irish tradition of the 'grush' is defined as 'a scramble by children to get coins or other small gifts thrown at them'. When children ran up to Byrne, he doled out sweets – bulldogs, perhaps, lollipops or lemon drops – as a way to produce a public sensation. At that time, sweets were among the few accessible luxuries in Free State Ireland, and domestic production increased in the 1930s, after Fianna Fáil put a tariff on English imports. Unlike most pleasures, eating candy was not then considered a mortal sin; chocolate and ice-cream were even marketed for their nutritional value. The reader who remembers Alfie Byrne may also recall the taste of Peggy's Leg. This toffee with brown sugar, syrup and molasses was made by Lemon's of Drumcondra. Other brands included Noblett's and B. B. toffee, advertised with a husband and wife eating separate boxes of toffee under the headline 'How to be happy though married'. All the ills of Dublin were once cured with a Melancholy Baby (vanilla ice-cream, red jelly, chocolate sauce, hundreds and thousands, and a blob of whipped cream). Byrne loved sweet things, and he also liked an audience. The weakness became its own solution, as the Pied Piper of Dawson Street led the children of Dublin on a dance for over thirty years.

On Sundays, Byrne woke up in the Mansion House, put on his morning suit, had breakfast with his wife, read the papers and went to Mass in the Pro-Cathedral. Then he met his older brother Lar and some other pals under Clerys clock on O'Connell Street. A street-trader, seeing the Lord Mayor there one day, went down on one knee, sweating the words, 'Oh my Lordship, my Lordship!' Byrne restored the woman to her feet and said, 'It's Alfie to you, as usual, Sally.' She pointed to a bag of potatoes and said, 'Give us a hand with these spuds, *Alfie.*' Like many stories that are told about Byrne, this may be apocryphal, even as it speaks to something authentic; in this case, a mixture of grandeur and self-effacement. The latter is a local speciality.

'You can always recognise a native Dubliner by his self-deprecation,' wrote Olivia Robertson. 'That habit he has acquired even more strongly than the ex-public school man. It is a habit which is fatal to promotion prospects in America, but in Dublin is essential, as it wards off possible criticism.'[6] That trait explains why Byrne could tell voters: 'I have had some successes and I have had my failings and shortcomings, but you have been kind enough to overlook them in the past, and I am hopeful that you will do so again.'[7] Another staple admission: 'I claim no deeds of great statesmanship to my credit – these are for more able than I.' And when jokes were made about his appearance, he refused to complain, saying, 'I like [them]. It is generally good stuff, well done, and I would feel very lonely if the humourists neglected me.'

They did not. Maureen Potter found fame by impersonating Byrne in the Gaiety pantomime, but it was her stage partner, Jimmy O'Dea, who coined the most enduring nickname: The Shaking Hand of Dublin. His eternal canvassing was a gift for comedians. 'There are three hands in the Byrne family crest – because Alfie needs a spare one.' What about the blaggard up in court for not signalling a right turn on his bicycle? 'When the judge asked him why he didn't put out his hand, he said, "I was afraid Alfie was going to shake it."'[8]

The Lord Mayor once boasted about being descended from the Byrnes of Wicklow, before adding that Byrne 'is the commonest name in Ireland'.[9] He often sent his chauffeur away from events, preferring to take the tram or the bus home.[10] As a seven- or eight-year-old child in the 1940s, Lochlann Quinn – who would become a prominent businessman, and whose son Oisín would serve as Lord Mayor of Dublin in 2013–14 – took the bus home from Belvedere

College one day. 'I remember telling my parents about a man who sat beside me and talked with me for part of the journey,' recalls Quinn. 'They asked me to describe him – he was a bit like Charlie Chaplin, with a cane or walking stick – and when I finished they both said, "That was Alfie Byrne!"' The Lord Mayor enjoyed meeting people in this way, and if his audience was gobsmacked by the resplendence of his costume, he would say, 'Call me Alfie.'

Byrne's appointments started at 10 a.m. and rarely finished before midnight. He did not appreciate the value of recreation. 'To do the job properly,' he once said of being a politician, 'is to work ten hours a day and be home to all-comers.'[11] He was a fan of Shamrock Rovers, but even this pastime acquired a professional dimension – he became vice-president of the Hoops – and he was also associated with another big team, Bohemians. There was political logic in this dual allegiance, as soccer was very popular. In 1911, there were thirty-one playing pitches in the Phoenix Park. Twenty-nine were used for soccer; just two were used for Gaelic football. (In the Dáil in 1926, Byrne asked the Minister for Finance to restore the cricket grounds beside the Wellington Monument.)[12]

Byrne's interest in soccer and his self-styled role as peacemaker were combined in the first crisis of his mayoralty, when three Bohemians players were suspended for taking part in an amateur match between Ireland and England in Belfast. At the time, there were rival soccer associations north and south, both claiming to represent the whole island. Byrne asked that the suspension of the players be lifted and legal proceedings stopped. The *Irish Independent* reported that he favoured 'a fifty-fifty agreement so far as international matches are concerned between the Northern and Southern bodies'.[13] Byrne's intervention was unsuccessful, and the relationship between the two bodies remained vexed for several decades.

In the 1930s, the Irish were insatiable readers of newspapers. With the exception of Éamon de Valera, who launched a newspaper to spread his own gospel, Byrne played the press better than any other politician of his generation. He treated pressmen like esteemed clients, he knew there was no point leaking good news at a time when the attention of the public was consumed by some momentous event, and even when he said the wrong thing, it only added to his colourful reputation. On one occasion, he apparently promised to put shoes on the footless (though that charming piece of Dublin humour may have its roots in a Jimmy O'Dea sketch).

When a monoplane was exhibited at Baldonnel airfield, he climbed into the machine for a short flight in strong winds and rain. The pilot asked if he really wanted to make the trip. 'Certainly,' he said. 'I always wondered what it was like in one of these things in bad weather. Now I can find out.' After the flight, he said 'airmindedness' was a thing of the future.[14] This image of Alfie Byrne as the gallant stuntman of Irish politics soon took hold in the public imagination. Why would the Lord Mayor stand with a pair of scissors to open Butt Bridge when he could cycle over the bridge and cut the ribbon at top speed, followed by several hundred other cyclists?

When the town of Clones, in Monaghan, was engulfed in a fire one night in December 1930, Dublin Fire Brigade offered to assist. The Lord Mayor donned a protective uniform and took a seat on the fire engine as it left Dublin for Clones. The image made for a popular cartoon that Christmas.[15] On returning to the capital, Byrne claimed, 'I have had one of the thrills of my life.' The fire engine had, he said, 'created excitement in the several towns through which we dashed. We reached Dundalk in an hour and eight minutes. We touched seventy miles an hour in some places.'[16] As if to prove that news travels fast, the reported speed of the fire engine soon increased. By that weekend, it was not seventy but eighty miles an hour.[17]

That Christmas, Byrne attended so many functions that one hack wondered if he ever found time to eat dinner. Out he went, talking up Dublin and Ireland, in that order. With ceremonial mace and sword, in those famous gold chains of office, the Lord Mayor lent foppish grandeur to parties, company dinners, gala balls and club dances all over the city. In a phrase that would please any barman, he was 'indefatigable in well-doing and courtesies'.[18]

Byrne's signature get-up was largely established by the time he became Lord Mayor, but something was still missing. In the first of seven appearances on the cover of *Dublin Opinion*, he had no facial hair. Making a return in January 1931, the twiddly moustache distracted attention from the poor condition of Byrne's front teeth; and though the teeth were upgraded in 1934, he kept the facial hair until the very end.

The overdressed mayor soon became a source of civic pride. His appeal transcended class and geography, and the elderly – particularly women – became fiercely proud of Byrne, spawning a mythology for their children and grandchildren. Indeed, this elusive figure is perhaps most legible as a Dublin street character like Bang Bang or Zozimus. Someone who Dubs were happy to see, Byrne made them feel good about living in the place. Better still, he gave them a voice. Before *Liveline*, there was Alfie Byrne.

Like any good comic-book hero, Byrne was first to the

scene of every disaster. On the night of 11–12 January 1931, a water main burst at the junction of Macken Street and Hogan Place, instantly making fifty people homeless. Byrne opened the Mansion House to those affected and gave them shelter, food and clothes. (He probably cannot be blamed for the fact that, in a 1961 article about him, the fifty householders became 'two hundred tormented homes, where water lapped coldly about the furniture'. It may even be true that Byrne 'fed the pitiable Dubliners for a fortnight at his own expense'.)[19]

Later that year, when floods hit parts of Dublin and Bray, Byrne was quick to respond once again, 'spending all night touring the hard-hit areas, sympathising, organising, encouraging'.[20] The prime minister, W. T. Cosgrave, presented a cheque for £1,000 as the government contribution to Byrne's relief fund. Flooding was a perennial problem in poorer areas of the city, another physical symptom of the housing crisis. When Drumcondra became the latest victim, the occupants of fourteen cottages were forced to leave their homes in the early hours. The *Irish Independent* reported that children were scantily dressed, 'and forced either to remain standing on the beds, or wade out to the streets, where they spent the remainder of the night'. Byrne offered sympathy and bags of coal, 'for drying their houses'.[21]

The Lord Mayor's reputation as a soft touch soon produced a joyless sight. Every morning, ten or fifteen men and women queued up outside the Mansion House. Most had hard-luck stories about money, disputes, health, housing, jobs or family, and all imagined the Lord Mayor could provide satisfaction. Byrne was a showman who conspired in the cultivation of his own legend, but he was not omnipotent, and eventually he was forced to admit as much.

There is an idea prevalent amongst a large number of people that the Mansion House is a sort of court of appeal from all other authorities. These people have had their cases tried with results that have been disappointing, or are burdensome. There are some whose claims for old age pension have been rejected, or who have failed to secure unemployment allowances, or they are anxiously seeking work. They have tried elsewhere and failed; then they come to me in numbers daily, thinking I can do something for them.[22]

A critic once said, 'No one knows better than Alfie what appeals to the man in the street, particularly the man who does not have to pay the bill.'[23] But the poor had few more diligent advocates. In January 1931, Byrne told the *Irish Times* that many Dubliners 'are in dire distress for fear of the loss of their homes. In the District Courts you can see them day by day pleading against notices to quit. A father and mother with two children get a food ticket worth 8s, and 2s, 6d. in cash, but it is insufficient to pay the rent of the room. Where are they to get the rent?'[24] The following month, a reporter from the *People* sat in Byrne's office while he dictated his morning letters. In less than an hour, he accepted seventeen invitations to dinners, one invitation to a play and eight invitations to public functions, in addition to dictating 'forty-three sympathetic letters to men and women looking for employment'. Byrne claimed to receive more than one hundred such appeals every day.[25]

Byrne's reputation quickly spread far beyond Dublin. A story in the *Irish Times* reported that he spent more money on postage in a week than any four of his predecessors combined. The article, headed 'Lord Mayor's Postbag: 15,000 letters', also formalized a nickname: 'The letters come from all of the earth, and often from people who know nothing about Ireland. One letter, whose contents showed it was intended for the Lord Mayor of Dublin, was addressed: "The Lord Mayor of Ireland, Sligo".[26]

Byrne liked to spread good news before it became official. One morning, he told some lads outside the Customs House, 'You boys need a bench.' That afternoon it magically appeared. (It was a much later Lord Mayor, Michael O'Halloran, who remembered that piece of Dublin folklore.) When Byrne got in the habit of boarding mail boats to welcome distinguished visitors to Dún Laoghaire, a Fianna Fáil councillor complained that the Lord Mayor 'comes out here to usurp our chairman's functions'. The chairman concurred: 'I have generally succeeded in being first on the boat, but not having any insignia of office except perhaps a temperance badge, I am not as easily recognizable as a man with links of gold round his neck. I have always preceded him, but he has always managed to get in his speech first.'[27]

Byrne's next party in the Mansion House featured 5,000 cakes, 2,500 sandwiches, 3,000 apples, 3,000 bananas and a ton of ice-cream.[28] Entertainment was provided by the Artane Band and acrobatic troupe and the St James's Band. W. T. Cosgrave gave a speech, provoking a furious response from the *Irish Press*. In a piece headlined 'How Alfie and Willie Use the Children', de Valera's newspaper thundered:

> What right has [Byrne] to mar the evening's pleasure of these children and their parents by intruding himself upon them in his political aspect? Can we not give our children a cup of tea in public without producing political skeletons at the feast! This is one instance of the brazen arts of humbuggery to which we are treated, and which we tolerate. There are many such enacted every week.[29]

While Byrne enchanted the youth of Dublin, the Children's Lord Mayor was largely absent as a father. 'We didn't see that much of him,' says Patrick Byrne. Cissie often took the children on holiday without their father, and Patrick never saw him in anything other than a stiff collar. There is a photo of Alfie Byrne on the beach with his family. He is dressed for City Hall. Chauffeur Bob Burton and another member of the team, Jim Reed, who welcomed visitors to the Mansion House, were prominent figures in the life of the Byrne children. When they played lawn tennis in the garden of the Mansion House, it was usually with one of their father's staff.

Byrne's first term as elected Lord Mayor came to an end that summer. Determined to retain the title, he set about securing support for his candidacy within Dublin City Council. Once again, he brokered the support of Cumann na nGaedheal in return for his fealty in the national parliament. He was, as Anne Dolan observes, 'the embodiment of political brokerage, balancing earnest endeavours on behalf of his constituents with his own political advancement'.[30]

At the meeting in City Hall on 1 July 1931, his nomination was proposed by Laurence O'Neill. When Martin O'Sullivan of Labour was also proposed, the meeting descended into chaos. Jim Larkin lambasted Labour, with whom he was feuding, and said the Lord Mayor's salary should be used to build houses. His words were drowned by cries from the public gallery: 'Where's it going already – out of Alfie's pocket!'[31] When someone else said Larkin would have pocketed the salary, Larkin called him a blackguard, before turning on Byrne, who had, he said, prostituted his position by sending congratulatory cards to people who had got a house from the Corporation. Eventually, Larkin and three of his supporters walked out of the council chamber.

The *Belfast Newsletter* noted that the loudest opposition to Byrne's re-election was 'from Larkinite and other Labour representatives, who are extremely jealous of "Alfie's" great popularity in the poor quarters of the city'.[32] The paper described Byrne as 'a curious study, because apart from his public position he is an absolute nobody. He is unlearned – he is not a big business man; he is not a politician.' The legend that he was 'non-political' was self-perpetuated, but the same piece also identified something genuine: 'If you meet him in the street, a dapper little man walking with quick steps, you feel sure that the friendly smile on his face was meant for you. Only the bitterest fanatics can withstand his friendliness. The friendliness is not mere show; "Alfie" has helped hundreds of lame dogs over stiles.'[33]

Byrne presented himself as a simple man with simple desires. All he wanted was jobs, housing, a united Ireland, more playgrounds, Mass on Sunday and a full dance card. It was not the world's most credible manifesto, and some of those goals would remain beyond his reach. But for now, at least, he was still on top.

On 1 July 1931, Alfie Byrne was re-elected for a second term as Lord Mayor of Dublin.

6. The Bleeding-Heart Racket

'In gambling, the many must lose in order
that the few may win.'

George Bernard Shaw

The tenements of Dublin bedevilled the state-building project. In the years following independence, housing conditions for the working classes of the city were among the worst in Europe, and life expectancy was heavily correlated with neighbourhood and class.[1] Byrne once had occasion to champion the cause of two families – a total of sixteen people – who lived in a single room of a Dublin tenement. He often attacked landlords who made it difficult for the Corporation to buy up such properties in order to demolish them, because they were demanding too high a price for the land. In some cases, he claimed, tenements were more expensive than houses on Merrion Square.[2]

Byrne spent much of the winter of 1931–2 working to relieve congestion in the tenements. 'Every member of the Corporation,' he said, 'is inspired by the one idea of clearing the slums and providing housing accommodation, and they are working practically day and night in their efforts to do so.' In the twelve months since the new Corporation had come into being, it had built two thousand houses, 'and the Housing Committee and the city manager have set their minds on building at the rate of 2,000 houses a year'.[3] In fact, over the next eight years, the rate was just shy of a thousand a year.

The Corporation proposed to tackle the related problems of housing and unemployment by paying unemployed men to clear derelict sites, so that houses could replace slum dwellings.[4] In 1931, the Corporation agreed to spend up to £25,000 on relief schemes, and called on the government to make a grant in order that the work be carried out.[5] Byrne was an enthusiastic promoter of such initiatives.

In the years following independence, Dublin was the only county in which women outnumbered men, largely because women from the countryside stood a greater chance of prospering in the capital than at home.[6] Byrne appealed to young people outside Dublin to stay there, because their friends had 'come here to find work and only got stranded'.[7] He said most homes in the tenement districts were bare of everything except for pictures, which the pawnbrokers refused to take. Men were lounging at street corners, too dispirited to return to their hungry families and fireless homes. 'The situation is horrible,' said Byrne. 'It has worried me more in the past few weeks than it ever has before.' He implored the Minister for Finance to ask for a relief grant 'of from £50,000 to £100,000 to help tide us over the crisis'.

The Great Depression made it difficult for municipalities to borrow money in order to build housing. In 1931, Byrne helped to organize a loan of £35,000 from the Royal Liver Friendly Society, of which he was now a senior trustee, to fund the building of houses by Bray Urban District Council. The *Irish Times* noted with approval that it was 'the third loan secured for public bodies through the Lord Mayor's influence. It is understood that similar applications have been made by other bodies.'[8] This sort of behaviour might be regarded as unethical today, but in the early 1930s Byrne's role as a broker presented no issue. Indeed, it was cited as a point in his favour by his fellow councillor Patrick Belton when nominating him for the mayoralty in 1936.

Byrne's facilitation of loans to build Corporation housing was not the only instance in which he used questionable methods to achieve useful ends. He was also an early champion of the Irish Hospitals' Sweepstake, a new racing-based lottery established in 1930 to fund the construction and modernization of hospitals. A teetotal publican who loves God and gambling cannot be said to have a straightforward moral compass. The story of Byrne's work for the Sweepstake is typical of a man whose personal interests overlapped, and sometimes conflicted with, his role as a public representative. It also illustrates two key weaknesses: his acquisitiveness and his fondness for spectacle.

Byrne's ability to raise money for good causes became evident during the Great War. When a merchant ship, the SS *Hare*, was torpedoed by a German U-boat about seven miles east of the Kish Lighthouse, Byrne and Richard Duggan, a well-known Dublin bookmaker, entered the charity numbers game. The lottery they organized together raised 'the fabulous sum of £3,000' for the families of the crew.[9] The following year, Duggan raised a thousand pounds for victims of another atrocity, when RMS *Leinster* was torpedoed by a German submarine. Then Byrne organized the Harbour Sweep in the spring of 1920. It raised £100 for deprived local children.[10]

In 1930, Richard Duggan asked the Lord Mayor for his help to promote the Irish Free State Hospitals' Sweepstake. Duggan was now working with Joe McGrath, a former member of the IRA, who had an extensive network of contacts in the United Kingdom, Canada and the United States, where such lotteries were illegal. That network would later prove useful as a way to promote the scheme. The third partner was a Welsh-born engineer, Captain Spencer Freeman.

The sweepstake was a lottery in which tickets were drawn at random, then assigned to a horse that was expected to run in a big race such as the Derby or the Grand National. If your ticket was drawn, and if it was assigned to a fast horse, you stood a fair chance of winning. Byrne was happy to talk up the venture, even hosting the launch event in the Mansion House. Demand for tickets for the inaugural sweep-stake was so great that at one time there were queues nearly a mile long outside the sweepstake offices in Dublin, and large numbers of police were detailed to steward them. At last the hospitals of Dublin would, said Byrne, be able to buy up-to-date equipment, 'so the city will have the best and most efficient hospitals in the world'.[11]

Encouraging the poor to gamble may seem a questionable use of the Lord Mayor's office, but Byrne said there was nothing wrong with 'selling anticipation'. He was confident that it would do no harm: 'I'm sure the morals of my people are not endangered by the Sweepstakes, nor is any needy household deprived of a single shilling.'[12]

The Catholic Church had an equally muddled attitude. The *Catholic Bulletin* once described the Sweepstake as 'a malignant menace, a putrid pool, a giant evil', and many priests railed against it. But another publication, the *Catholic Mind*, ran large ads for the Sweepstake and, when a woman asked the agony aunt in a Jesuit journal if it was okay to pray to win the Sweep, she was told there was nothing wrong with the wealth that a prize brings, 'but don't forget what Our Lord said about the camel'.[13] The reader was encouraged to pray for a prize, 'because then you can be sure that you won't win it if it is going to do harm to your soul'.[14] Further, many Catholic clergy were enthusiastic proponents of sweepstakes as a source of funds for a good cause – including, of course, Church-controlled hospitals.

In toasting the success of the first Sweepstake, Byrne claimed – somewhat ludicrously – that the initiative would 'come to the rescue of the slums of Ireland, from which most of the hospital patients came'.[15] Due to massive media and public interest, the Mansion House was too small to host the second sweep, so it was held in the ballroom of a hotel. Byrne took turns drawing the tickets with the Garda Commissioner, General Eoin O'Duffy.

The promoters said the cost of running the lottery would not exceed 9 per cent of the subscriptions, and that hospitals would receive £735,463 from the second sweep. In reality, only a fraction of the money raised went to good causes, though this did not become widely known until much later. As Stephen Dodd has written, 'While the betting operation purported to be run for charity – and underlined the notion at every turn by using nurses and gardai to lend legitimacy to draws – its true purpose was to create huge profits for a core of influential schemers.'[16] Reader's Digest once described the Sweepstake as 'the greatest bleeding-heart racket in the world'.[17]

In the early years, up to three quarters of Sweepstake tickets were sold in Britain. As Marie Coleman has written, 'In effect, during the early 1930s the Irish hospital service was financed by private individuals living in Britain, making a mockery of Fianna Fáil's drive for self-sufficiency.'[18] The British authorities brought in legislation to stem the flow of money, and the raffle further exacerbated tensions between the British and Irish governments at a time of economic depression.[19] Byrne, for his part, continued to talk up the Sweepstake for many years. In 1935, he chided an American pressman for neglecting to ask him about 'one of our principal industries – the Irish Sweepstakes'. Byrne boasted, 'We have erected one of the best hospital systems in the world, Germany and America included. We are now opening the finest maternity hospital in Europe, and many hospitals have been opened in various parts of Ireland through this fund.' Asked if the lottery placed a burden on the poor, he said, 'No, it does not, but it builds fine hospitals.'[20]

The Lord Mayor had a selfish reason to make such bullish claims: he was a ticket agent for the Sweepstake. Byrne employed a man called Christy Hendrick to sell tickets from an office above Morgan's wine shop, across the road from the Mansion House.[21] Such arrangements were common at the time, and Byrne was not the only politician in hock to the promoters of the Sweepstake. Other TDs, including leading figures in Fianna Fáil, Fine Gael and Labour, were bankrolled by the organization, which paid for deposits at elections and made donations for campaign expenses.[22] But Byrne's position was further complicated by his own pretensions. He once explained the fact that he didn't have a ticket in the drum by saying that he 'did not think people who were concerned in the drawing should have any personal financial interest in it'.[23] As we have seen, the Lord Mayor was rather more complex than his folksy image suggested. Perhaps it is useful to think of him not merely as a political showman but as a businessman with a hatful of good numbers: ticket agent, PR man, stock-picker, trustee and first citizen.

The Irish Hospitals' Sweepstake continued to enrich its backers for decades. In his memoir of Dublin in the mid-twentieth century, John Ryan wrote that Joe McGrath, the most prominent of the men behind the Sweeps, went around in a chauffeur-driven Rolls-Royce, kept strings of racehorses, smoked big cigars and 'wore an outrageous white golf cap'. McGrath was, by government appointment, the first millionaire in the Free State. 'Having had the franchise of the Irish Hospital Sweepstakes given to him, he was in the position of a man who is given a colour offset lithographic machine by the authorities with the injunction: "Now go ahead and print all the five pound notes you need." '[24]

The Sweepstake played a prominent role in Irish life until the 1980s, when dwindling revenues and allegations of financial chicanery finally brought it to a halt. At this remove, it is arguable that the venture embodied some of the worst aspects of public life in Ireland: the privatization of what should be public functions; the false veneer of charity; the corruption; and the self-serving hypocrisy of the Church and the political establishment.

Alfie Byrne was among the earliest and loudest champions of this gigantic wheeze.

7. Nibbling Carrots and the Rise of Fianna Fáil

Alfie Byrne was re-elected to the Senate in the election of December 1931. In the run-up to the election, he had also canvassed for his mentor, Laurence O'Neill. Some of Byrne's erstwhile allies felt that his endorsement of O'Neill had caused the defeat of a Cumann na nGaedheal candidate, George Crosbie. In the Byrne archive, there is a handwritten note scrawled on a brown envelope. Addressed to 'President Cosgrave', the message reads:

> Some have said that my eagerness to secure Senator O'Neill's return to Senate interfered with Mr Crosbie's possible election. I would be very sorry to think so. Crosbie's splendid work in [the] National Cause for [the] past quarter of a century and my admiration for same tempts me to make the following suggestion: that I will resign my seat and you kindly invite him to accept it, we might be able to arrange a unanimous election.[1]

The offer was accepted by Cosgrave, and it won Byrne new admirers in the government. This was but the latest chapter in the political dance between Byrne and Cumann na nGaedheal. It was classic Alfie: ostensibly noble, but also self-serving. It would not have escaped Byrne's attention that Crosbie's family owned the *Cork Examiner*, while Cosgrave knew that Crosbie's elevation to the Senate would remove a potential rival in his Cork constituency.

In January 1932, the press speculated that Byrne could

succeed James McNeill as Governor-General, the king's representative in the Free State. The salary for the position was an extraordinary £10,000 a year, and the post came with a grand, state-maintained residence in the Phoenix Park, the Viceregal Lodge.[2] As an Anglophile and a lover of wealth, status and extravagant parties, the rumour must have tickled Byrne. But W. T. Cosgrave had another plan.

At the end of January, Cosgrave dissolved the Dáil, partly in order to avoid any chaos during the Eucharistic Congress later that year.[3] The election looked tricky for a somewhat lethargic Cumann na nGaedheal, up against a well-organized and energetic Fianna Fáil. At the start of the campaign, the *Derry Journal* speculated that Byrne would have to shore up Cosgrave's hold on a vital constituency:

> North Dublin is presenting a knotty crux. Cumann na nGaedheal has at present six of the seats but two of these were secured at by-elections by narrow majorities which were made up largely of the postal votes of soldiers serving in the Free State Army. The party knows that it will be a different proposition in a general election, and it has, I understand, made up its mind that it is going to lose one of the seats. It is doubtful about holding the second, and the delay in having a convention is due to its hunt for a strong man with good 'local pull'. There is a possibility that our old friend, the Lord Mayor, Dublin's champion hand-shaker, will be prevailed upon to do the needful for the party.

In a letter that was written to be published in the national press, Cosgrave called on his old friend Byrne to run for the Dáil:

In the interests of the people of the city, who love you so well, and to whom you have devoted the best years of your life with patriotic disinterestedness, I earnestly appeal to you to come forward as a candidate for the Dáil at the coming general election, to add one more act of citizenship to the many already to your credit.

Addressing his response to 'My dear President', Byrne nibbled at the carrot. This letter was also published in the national press:

As you know, when I resigned from the Seanad I stated in the most definite manner that I was not, and would not, be a candidate for the Dáil. You are aware that during the past three weeks I have rigidly adhered to this position, and refused every request to allow myself to be nominated, and that you were included amongst those who were reluctantly refused. I have been thinking for some time, and am still of the same opinion, that after my rather strenuous work extending over a quarter of a century I might reasonably look forward to a period of rest and ease from the worries, troubles and difficulties incidental to public life in Ireland.

And then he continued to nibble:

Long continued thought on your letter, and our conversation arising from your message to meet you at Longford, make it appear to me that you and your colleagues consider that the ensuing general election is one of momentous importance to us all, that on its results depends the future of the Free State, and by that I mean the happiness and prosperity of the general body of the people, I recognise fully that any change of Government now, and the election of a new one pledged to uproot the magnificent foundations laid by you during the last ten years, mean for Dublin a continuation of slums, great risks for those in shaky employment, a development of unemployment, and an increase in poverty and misery generally; and that for the whole country it means uncertainty, bad trade, bad prices for produce, and the whole State going continuously backward in place of forward.

After more nibbling:

You seem to think that if I consent to be a candidate for Dublin North my old and faithful friends will rally round me in such numbers as to make it positively certain that Dublin will again definitely declare itself as a strong supporter of the Treaty and your Government, and you apparently believe that such a result would be of enormous advantage to you in the appeal now being made to the citizens of the Free State.

Finally, Alfie Byrne ate the whole carrot.

The issues suggested by you are so big that I find it impossible to adhere to my personal desires, and thus feel compelled to accept your request as a national command. I will be nominated to-day, and will issue a strong appeal to all my friends for the support of the government candidates, and will do my very best to impress on those who were absent at the last voting the importance of this occasion and the dangers of abstention on the sixteenth.

Byrne's decision to run for the Dáil – and the dramatic exchange of letters – was one of the most talked-about aspects of the short campaign. As one commentator observed, 'Alfie is not a party man, and when he said he would lend a hand to

President Cosgrave there was a minor sensation. In Dublin he carries more weight than any three other men.'[4] Despite his public expression of support for the government, Byrne – who was mindful, no doubt, of his experience in 1918 – ran as an Independent, urging his voters to give their preferences to General Richard Mulcahy and the other Cumann na nGaedheal candidates. In a circular published shortly before the election, 'What Your Vote Means', he explained his position with unusual brevity:

Every vote for the Government is a vote for:

1. The Treaty and our sense of honour as a nation;
2. Quiet continuous improvement in all kinds of business from agriculture to our factories;
3. Gradual creation of happiness for our people based upon sound Christian principles and material comfort.

Every vote for Mr de Valera's candidates is a vote for:

1. Breaking the Treaty;
2. The creation of turmoil and trouble; dread uncertainty; stagnation in trade; unemployment and misery.

On the day before the dissolution of the Dáil, W. T. Cosgrave addressed a party convention that Byrne hosted in the Mansion House. It was a nasty election campaign, in which violence sometimes broke out at pro-government election rallies. In College Green, Cosgrave's platform was guarded by serried ranks of civic guards, and, according to the *Fermanagh Herald*, 'others were drawn up at intervals all round College Green. But from the opening of his meeting to its close somebody was fighting somebody else somewhere in the crowd.' A candidate, Dr Thomas Hennessy, collapsed on the platform, and for ten minutes, 'while the crowd remained hushed, Hennessy lay with a mortally sick appearance in the arms of friends'. Byrne succumbed to the emotion of the occasion: 'A priest and doctor hastened to [Hennessy's] side, and in the most critical moment of the attack the Dublin Lord Mayor, Senator Alfie Byrne, burst into tears.'[5] When de Valera addressed Fianna Fáil supporters on the same spot the next evening, he 'spoke in profound silence interrupted only by great waves of spontaneous applause'.[6]

The *Daily Mail* reported: 'One candidate said with typical inconsequence, "The women of Dublin seem to have voted to a man."' This may be the origin of the quip that 'the women of Dublin vote for Alfie to a man'. Still, there was nothing laughable about the candidate's performance. Byrne got 18,170 first-preference votes. For the second time in five years, the housewives' darling had secured the largest poll of any candidate in the country.

After the election, the *Derry Journal* teased out the back-story to Byrne's very public flirtation with Cumann na nGaedheal:

> The dramatic correspondence on the eve of the election between 'My Dear Lord Mayor' and 'My Dear President' was simply stage play to deceive the groundlings. The whole business was fixed up a month before. The Government decided to label Alfie 'Independent' – why I don't know. It didn't throw dust in anybody's eyes here and to the 18,000 odd who voted for him it mattered not one thraneen . . . They vote for the man himself.[7]

Cosgrave's gambit worked in north Dublin, but he lost the

election. Fianna Fáil won a plurality of seats and formed a government with the support of the Labour Party; Éamon de Valera took office as President of the Executive Council. W. T. Cosgrave would spend the rest of his career on the opposition benches. Byrne had a seat in the Dáil, but his access to the Cabinet was now completely cut off.

Less than a decade on from the civil war, Cosgrave and de Valera ensured that there was a peaceful transfer of power. When the new Dáil met for the first time, a sketchwriter from the London *Evening Standard* was there – alongside many members of the public, including women with babies in their arms – to capture the scene:

> I stared hard at de Valera and his men. They are not an inspiring sight. As statesmen they look the amateurs they actually are. They are nervous and unready. De Valera himself has an unauthoritative air. His beak-like nose and long lips and the lump of black hair hanging on his forehead shows the fanatic, but he speaks haltingly and his manner is that of an amiable bank clerk. Much more striking were the men in back benches behind him, his thorny support. They made the Dáil resemble a trade union meeting. Here were many Irish country types; men with great bunches of hair like clumps of grass growing from the fronts of their heads; men black of brow and eyes and hair; hard-faced men.[8]

This was the new establishment. Determined to get along, even as he held his nose, Byrne declared his loyalty to the new government 'in any effort they may make to fulfil their election promise to the unemployed and all those who believe they are being injured by being asked to carry out unfair business'.[9] However, he would refuse to support de Valera on any bill that would change the Constitution or the Treaty.

Turning to the opposition benches, the *Evening Standard* correspondent noted that William Cosgrave, 'small and blond, is what we should call a House of Commons man. He had but to speak to make me know that here was a man used to authority.' Behind him sat 'the Lord Mayor, a small man, half-hiding his chain of office under his jacket; and John Dillon's son, cold and collegiate, and John Redmond's son, with his father's nose.'[10] All the heirs of Home Rule Ireland, together in a Dublin parliament. Byrne in the chain from William of Orange. Wing collars. Patent leather shoes.

No one expected the government to last.

Alfie Byrne was fifty years old on 14 March 1932. There was no birthday party, and it is unlikely that he did much celebrating. In addition to his political and business commitments, he was busy preparing for the Eucharistic Congress, the most extravagant religious spectacle in Irish history. The Congress was a very public expression of religious authority. In Byrne, it had the perfect host.

That spring, he arranged for the horse-drawn coach used by previous Lord Mayors, including Daniel O'Connell, to be restored, so that it could be used to transport the Papal Legate through the city. That link to O'Connell, who provided the money to establish Byrne's school, would have pleased Byrne no end. (He once went to visit a centenarian on her birthday, because she had met the Liberator and now wanted to shake the hand of Alfie Byrne.[11]) To lend the occasion even more pageantry, he revived the tradition of wearing ceremonial robes.[12] This was a conscious enlarging of the office of Lord Mayor, as well as an attempt to lend it some O'Connell-style razzmatazz. The opening of Butt Bridge served as a dress rehearsal for the new costumes, with

Byrne turning up – to much amusement – in a bright crimson robe.[13]

Byrne asked citizens to 'brush up Dublin' in time for the Congress, 'and now front doors and window frames that had become dingy with age are blossoming into brilliance'.[14] Floodlights were erected at the High Altar in Phoenix Park, four hundred loudspeakers were installed along the quays, and a special replica of a Norman gateway was erected at Merrion so that the Papal Legate could receive an impressive welcome.

To greet the Pope's representative, Cardinal Lorenzo Lauri, Byrne gave a grandiloquent oration that had none of the self-deprecation that peppered his best speeches:

> Before I ask the city manager to offer to you the sincerest welcome of our city, may I be permitted as Lord Mayor of Dublin, officially to express something of the sentiments that fill every heart today towards the august person of your Eminence ... Welcome to your Eminence, Legate of his Holiness, a hundred thousand welcomes to you in whom we have the honour to salute every successor of St Peter, the vicar of Christ Himself.

There was a carnival atmosphere in Dublin during the Congress. Twelve miles of bunting was strung along the streets, and searchlights illuminated the sky at night, while legislation was introduced to enable the sale of alcohol to guests staying on ships that were moored along the Liffey. Towards the end of the week, the Lord Mayor presented Cardinal Lauri with the Freedom of Dublin at a reception in the Mansion House. 'Your Eminence has secured a warm place in the hearts of the people of Dublin, of Ireland, and of the great Irish race beyond the seas,' he said. 'It is with feelings of great regret that we observe the approach of the hour when Your Eminence must depart from our shores.'[15] In response, the Legate said, 'Mr Mayor, I thank you with all my heart for the feelings of affection which you have manifested towards me and for the great honour which you conferred on me in nominating me as a citizen of this historical town.'[16]

The event was not as harmonious as these platitudes suggest. The trouble began when the Minister for Defence, Frank Aiken, said the army band would not play at the reception unless Byrne withdrew his invitation to the Governor-General, James McNeill.[17] This was a sign of the times: Fianna Fáil was seeking to undermine one of the pillars of the Anglo-Irish Treaty. When Byrne refused to withdraw the invitation to McNeill, the *Kerry News* reported, he was 'met with obstruction in quarters from which he should have received cordial co-operation. His application for a military guard of honour . . . was rejected in the most insolent manner.' Determined to get his way, Byrne asked Jim Larkin to send a trade union band to play. Patrick Byrne recalls that Larkin agreed on one condition: 'that the mayor would pay for the band's new uniforms'. Alfie was happy to oblige. For a modest sum, he would jolly up the party, build a bridge with Larkin, honour Dublin's connections with Rome and London, and stick it to the Fianna Fáil government.

De Valera was furious. According to the *Morning Post*, he 'tried to shoulder the Governor-General out of place alongside the Legate at the head of the procession into the Round Room, and was only prevented from doing so by the polite, but very firm, intervention of the Lord Mayor'.[18] Later that year, McNeill left the job, frustrated by the government's attempts to undermine his position.

The tenor John McCormack performed at the reception in

the Mansion House. He also sang 'Panis Angelicus' for a million people at the concluding Mass in Phoenix Park. 'It was just an infinity of men and women,' wrote the *Irish Times*, 'marshalled into their places with consummate skill; ordered, decent and reverent, setting an example to the world of popular piety, and behaving with a quiet dignity that was worthy of the occasion which evoked it.'[19]

Thousands of Dubliners gathered at Dún Laoghaire to bid farewell to Cardinal Lauri. The *Liverpool Echo* described the week as 'an unqualified success on the material as well as the spiritual side', adding that over £5 million had been spent during the Congress. Demonstrating that the Free State was a Catholic state for a Catholic people, the Congress was also a triumph for Byrne and for the role of Lord Mayor: a newly prominent and unimpeachable position in public life.[20] The mayor was strong, even with powerful enemies in government, because he had a gold chain, a crimson cloak and a horse-drawn carriage. No one could touch him that summer.

8. Dangerous Idiots

'You, the people, have the power to make this
life free and beautiful, to make this life a
wonderful adventure.'
Charlie Chaplin in *The Great Dictator*

In photographs, Alfie Byrne seems to have a stately demean-
our; but contemporary recollections evoke a man who was
small and frenetic. Opponents called him the Mansion
House Rat. The socialist activist Frank Ryan once described
Byrne even less flatteringly as a 'sewer-rat' in his newspaper,
Republican Congress: 'When Alfie periodically rediscovers the
slums, it doesn't mean that his conscience twinges at the
contrast between the empty rooms of the Mansion House
and the over-crowded slums. All it means is that Alfie knows
there's a need to go vote hunting.'

The truth is that Byrne spent his whole life hunting for
votes. What kept him going? Some politicians use the work to
feed the ego. In his case, the memory of poverty was probably
critical. For the Shaking Hand of Dublin, victories felt provi-
sional, and his eye was usually on tomorrow, because it brought
him one day closer to the next election. By 1933, he had four
jobs, seven children and a quarter of a million dependants.

Upon coming to power, Éamon de Valera started an Economic War against the United Kingdom, imposing trade
tariffs and halting the payment of land annuities dating back

to the Land Acts of the late nineteenth century. The Irish people were encouraged to 'burn everything English except their coal' – a phrase dating back to Jonathan Swift. Byrne, however, argued at every turn for better relations with Ireland's largest trading partner. In Wales that autumn he told a group of businessmen and politicians that idealists – 'people who have exaggerated views of nationality and patriotism' – were responsible. 'Tariffs on the one side and retaliation on the other side will not benefit your people or ours. The time has arrived to bring this crisis to an end for the benefit of both our peoples.'[1]

The Economic War made the conservatism of Irish life even more acute, as Terence Brown has observed: 'To cultural and religious protectionism at their most draconian in the censorship policy was added the official encouragement of economic nationalism as a force sustaining the structure of an essentially rural society dominated by the social, cultural, and political will of farmers and their offspring.'[2] Emigration seemed the best option for thousands of Dubliners, including Byrne's younger brother George, who tried to set himself up as a hairdresser in London.[3]

In September 1932, Byrne was elected as Lord Mayor of Dublin for a third time, defeating the widow of Tom Clarke, Senator Kathleen Clarke. Following the vote, Jim Larkin admitted that Byrne had 'brought to the Mansion House a spirit of comradeship and kindliness that was absent from it for many years'. Laurence O'Neill responded, 'I am delighted to hear Mr Larkin's tribute to Alderman Byrne, and I hope it is an indication of happier things to come.'

It was not.

One evening in December 1932, the Round Room of the Mansion House was reserved for a communist meeting.

Byrne took the unusual step of refusing to allow the event to take place. He reportedly 'bought a large chain and a heavy padlock, and himself securely chained the entrance gates, to prevent the ingress of any Communist'.[4]

James Larkin Jr moved a motion of censure against Byrne on the City Council. Then his father said, 'I suppose the Lord Mayor got his orders. The meeting was to celebrate the anniversary of the Russian Revolution, and because I happen to be one of those hated people known as communists I was refused permission to have it in the Mansion House and send greetings to Russian comrades.' This critique is more damning in retrospect because Byrne later attended and gave his blessing to a Blueshirt meeting in the same venue.

On 28 December 1932, Byrne hosted a meeting of 130 prominent citizens in the Mansion House. There it was agreed to host a conference at a later date 'to establish a political party in the Free State unifying all opinion which recognizes that the interests of the State are bound up within the Commonwealth'.[5] A senior figure in Cumann na nGaedheal told the *Irish Press* that his party 'would welcome the Lord Mayor's plan and that it would mean a massing of opposition. If Fianna Fáil did not agree with it he believed it would mean the overthrow of the Government'.[6]

Demanding an end to the Economic War, the cultivation of friendly relations with Britain, national unity and the full working of the Treaty, speakers at the meeting explored the appeal of a new party. Buoyed by his position at the centre of national affairs, Byrne abandoned any pretensions to independence, telling his audience that the country was faced with a grave crisis. 'Tradition must be put aside and public duty discharged.'[7]

The Mansion House Appeal contributed to the emergence, several months later, of Fine Gael – a new party created by a merger of Cumann na nGaedheal, the National Centre Party and the National Guard, aka the Blueshirts. Ciara Meehan has written that 'from the earliest stage, Alfie Byrne, the Lord Mayor of Dublin and legendary independent deputy, played an instrumental role in forging the notion of a new national party'.[8] And because of his machinations in this regard, Byrne was openly ridiculed by opponents in Fianna Fáil. Despite his nominal independence, he was, they said, a stooge for Cosgrave. Byrne denied the charge:

> I am not, and never have been, a member of the Cumann na nGaedheal Party. In the Dáil and Seanad I have from time to time criticised the Governments presided over by Mr Cosgrave, and voted against them. On several occasions, such actions resulted in unpleasant and what I considered to be unfair remarks about myself, but these little asides never prevented me from seeing perfectly clearly that Mr Cosgrave's Governments had done, and were doing, enormous work for the country. For Mr Cosgrave himself I always had a great personal regard, and admired his character, capacity and courage. On national questions I never had any difficulty following his lead. I could not forget that, in 1916, he had done his part, according to his view, that he was arrested in the uniform of the Volunteers, was tried by a drumhead court martial, and sentenced to death.[9]

While the main opposition party was considering its next move, de Valera seized the initiative by calling a snap election. Byrne issued a now-customary warning, as reported by the *Cork Examiner*: 'On Monday the Lord Mayor intimated to his [supporters] in the North City Constituency that their confidence in his popularity may be the undoing of him in the election ... [he] is taking no risks, and tells his friends that they must not drop him to No. 2.'[10]

During the election campaign, Byrne gave a bullish interview to the *Evening Mail*: 'Is now the time to show the white feather? No, a thousand times no. I will not take the easy way. Why should I run away?' He was 'not afraid of the flag-waver or the gun-bully or crowds who use their boots on candidates when darkness falls ... Mysterious assassins advised me to take care, as they had a bullet with my name on it ... They abused me for wearing the Lord Mayor's chain of office, yet it is the same chain that was worn by Daniel O'Connell, MP, when he was Lord Mayor in 1841.'

Byrne was easily re-elected to the national parliament, but on this occasion he secured fewer votes than his old rival Seán T. O'Kelly. This was in line with national trends: Fianna Fáil secured a working majority in the election, with seventy-seven seats, while Cumann na nGaedheal lost nine seats, bringing its total down to forty-eight.

In the 1930s, nine out of ten Irish people were practising Catholics. Bishops routinely issued broadsides against godless communism. To the minds of the faithful, the red threat was so real that extraordinary measures were needed to prevent the young from being corrupted.

Alfie Byrne's fear of communism was overblown and sometimes irrational, but that position was common. In October 1931, a bill – commonly called the Public Safety Act – was rushed through the Dáil to give the government the power to declare a state of emergency and take various security measures. Cosgrave immediately declared a state of emergency, and banned twelve organizations, including Saor

Éire and the IRA. A few days later, a meeting of the City Council descended into chaos when Fianna Fáil TD and councillor Robert Briscoe introduced a motion calling on the government to remove the legislation. Byrne retorted that Briscoe had had three days to share his views of the Bill in the Dáil, but had failed to do so. He was, said Byrne, 'trying to foment trouble by making wild speeches of attack on the State.'[11] The *Belfast Telegraph* takes up the story:

> The Lord Mayor immediately left the Chamber followed by the Corporation officials and the majority of the members of the Council. There was a storm of protest from the crowded galleries, and Councillor James Larkin, one of the signatories to the requisition, moved that the minority appoint a chairman to carry on. Amid cries of 'Up the Republic!' from the public galleries, Councillor Thomas Kelly was called to the chair and, in the appeal for order, stated that the meeting was not going to be turned into a rabble. Practically every one of the thirteen members constituting the minority remaining made a speech, in which the Lord Mayor and the Government were attacked in turn, and at the close a resolution condemning the action of the Lord Mayor, and protesting against the Act, was unanimously passed.

The situation deteriorated further, and later that month the government provided Byrne with an armed bodyguard. 'His Lordship does not want such protection,' reported the *Ulster Herald*, 'but the Government insists that he must have it.'[12]

Shortly after Fianna Fáil came to power, the new government ended the state of emergency and released a number of IRA prisoners. As the messy aftermath of the Civil War played itself out, a number of ex-servicemen formed the

Army Comrades Association (ACA), described by the historian Dermot Keogh as 'a quasi praetorian guard' for Cumann na nGaedheal, and by Diarmaid Ferriter as 'a movement designed, in theory, to protect freedom of speech and assembly and oppose the policies of Fianna Fáil'.[13]

The 1933 General Election saw ugly confrontations between supporters of Fianna Fáil or ex-members of the anti-Treaty IRA (whose slogan was 'No free speech for traitors') and the ACA. Byrne saw red. In an election leaflet, he asked: 'Have you noticed the breaking-up of public meetings in the city of Dublin by a cowardly mob which shrieks for free speech? Meaning free speech for themselves, not for you or me. Who are they? What are they after?'[14]

On election day, Byrne was verbally abused by three hardchaws outside a polling station. There was a brief scuffle before a policeman intervened. Byrne turned the handbags into headlines: 'He caught me by the coat and struck me on the back. [So] I struck out and hit him in the face.' Keep talking, Alfie. 'I had to defend myself, and much as I did not like to do so, had to hit the man who hit me.'[15] This piece of Dublin street pantomime was well received by the *Belfast Telegraph*: 'Mr Byrne is no longer in the prime of youth and is a small man, but he is full of pluck. To-day his chief difficulty, he confessed, was his responsibility of comporting himself and standing up for his rights as a good Irishman. Apparently he did both efficiently.'[16]

Shortly after this episode, Byrne told the republican paper *An Phoblacht* that Ireland was heading for ruin. The interview features the mixture of bluster and paranoia that characterizes many of his utterances during this period. 'The dark forces of Communism are ranged in their hordes behind Fianna Fáil,' he asserted. 'Their insidious propaganda is eating and will eat into the hearts of the Irish people.' When it was pointed out that communism had little support in Ireland, Byrne entered the frightening world of unknown unknowns.

> Ha! You are quite right, that just shows the cleverness of the communists. Their underhand methods are such that they do not give themselves away, they do not even try to spread their opinions in this country. Fianna Fáil does not realize the danger which exists, the people do not know, even the communists themselves do not know.

Standing, then, with his hand outstretched, Byrne said, 'But all is not yet lost. I myself will lead against this menace the forces of . . . of . . .'

'Of what?' said the reporter.

'The forces against the menace!'

In February 1933, de Valera sacked Eoin O'Duffy from his post as Garda Commissioner. Taking over as leader, O'Duffy had the ACA renamed as the National Guard and adopted a blue shirt as uniform. Determined to rid Ireland of 'communism and alien influence in national affairs, and to uphold Christian principles,' he toured the country on a recruitment campaign.

Concerned that O'Duffy might try to seize power, de Valera banned the National Guard. This prompted three parties – Cumann na nGaedheal, the Centre Party and the National Guard – to merge into a new organization, Fine Gael, in September 1933. O'Duffy was its first president, although Cosgrave remained leader of the parliamentary party. An irascible figure, O'Duffy became increasingly strident, even militaristic, alienating many of his new colleagues.

Byrne knew Eoin O'Duffy through their mutual involvement in the Sweepstake. O'Duffy's Blueshirts were 'clerico-fascist', in Dermot Keogh's term; more recently, Ferriter has described them as 'an economically disgruntled group, organised along parish and county lines with separate women's and children's divisions, utilising the trappings of fascism'.

Byrne was photographed giving a raised-arm salute at a meeting in the Round Room of the Mansion House in 1934.[17] (As we have seen, Byrne refused to allow a communist event to be held in the same venue.) The photo shows O'Duffy, president of Fine Gael, taking the salute from a large group, including Byrne and W. T. Cosgrave. In the memorable phrase of Padraig Yeates, Byrne looks 'more like a little boy asking permission to go to the toilet than a potential Irish strong-man'.[18] Does the photograph prove that Byrne was a fascist?

Anne Dolan, who wrote the *Dictionary of Irish Biography* entry on Alfie Byrne, stresses the danger of reading history backwards. 'Like many supporters of Cumann na nGaed-heal, and more so as it became Fine Gael, Byrne was seen at events where the one-armed salute adopted by the Blueshirts was practised. That does not make him a fascist or anti-Semite in and of itself.'[19] Another historian of the period, Mike Cronin, says of the picture, 'To conflate what we know of European fascism in the 1930s and apply this to anyone who was near the Blueshirts in the 1930s is bad history.'[20] Fearghal McGarry adds, 'Despite the shirt and raised-arm salute, few Blueshirts beyond a radical minority within the leadership embraced fascist ideas.'

Byrne was like many members of Fine Gael in that his support for O'Duffy was influenced by his determination to defeat the seemingly invincible de Valera. But there were other strands to this tendency in Irish politics. Byrne was sympathetic to some of the aims of fascist movements that emerged in Europe in the 1930s, because of his Catholicism and his antipathy to communism. When the Spanish Civil War started, it was widely regarded in Ireland as a battle between Christian virtue and communist evil.[21] Eoin O'Duffy organized an Irish brigade to fight on Franco's side (with shambolic results), and in December 1936 Byrne sent a message of support. O'Duffy read it out to his men 'at Church parade' on Christmas morning, and then wrote to Byrne:

> Believe me, of the many messages received none was more appreciated or more cordially applauded. On my own behalf and on behalf of every member of the Brigade I tender to your Lordship most sincere thanks. It was very kind of you to remember us here on this bleak mountain side far from our homes and those dear to us.[22]

In 1938, Byrne and de Valera were among the many worthies who welcomed two Italian naval training ships to Dublin. Byrne was politically allied to people like Patrick Belton and Oliver J. Flanagan, who were notorious for their anti-Semitism. In 1936, Byrne presided over a meeting of the Irish Christian Front, which was led by Belton, who once said, 'If the Jews do not conform to Christian ways, let them go back to Palestine.'[23] But this author has found no evidence that Byrne shared the despicable anti-Semitism of Belton or Flanagan. In fact, Byrne enjoyed a particularly good relationship with the Jewish community. In 1914, under the heading 'Alfy [sic] Byrne in a New Role', Jim Larkin's *Irish Worker* took the trouble to list Byrne's fellow shareholders in the George's Street Picture Palace, some of whom – Harris Wigoder, Bernard Glick, Mark Rubinstein – had Jewish-sounding names; the journalist and scholar Colum Kenny has called this an example of 'dog-whistle anti-Semitism'.[24] This was not inconsistent with the editorial policy of Larkin's paper, which published other articles that were effectively expressions of contempt for Jews. Later, Byrne received warm letters from Louis Elliman, the most prominent Jewish citizen in Dublin, and the 'Sinn Féin rabbi', Isaac Herzog.[25] He also gave the chairman of the council for the Jewish Agency for Palestine a civic welcome, opened a bazaar in the Mansion House in aid of the Jewish National Fund and supported the Orthodox synagogue.[26] Towards the very end of his life, he even officiated at the prize-giving in a school for the Jewish community.[27]

In response to a query from the author, the Jewish Representative Council of Ireland stated:

> Following our own inquiries among people who would have been familiar with the period, including those whose parents would have known Mr Byrne, we have found no evidence to support or suggest that Mr Alfie Byrne was anti-Semitic or ever behaved in a manner that offended the Jewish community during his life or years in office.

When Eoin O'Duffy and his men returned from the Spanish Civil War, the Lord Mayor welcomed them with a reception. But in 1939, Byrne declined to attend a Mass of thanksgiving for Franco's victory. When O'Duffy died in 1944, Byrne attended his funeral – as did Cosgrave and de Valera.

In Dublin, Alfie Byrne is not remembered as a fascist or an anti-Semite. However, with his short stature, funny moustache and frenzied appeals, it is inarguable that he resembled one well-known fascist leader. The tyrant in question was not Adolf Hitler, but Charlie Chaplin in the final scene of *The Great Dictator*: a misguided but fundamentally decent man in a world beset by dangerous idiots.

9. How You Play the Game

'To be a T.D. and to do the job properly is to work
ten hours a day and be home to all-comers, to listen
patiently, to guide and to advise those in difficulty, to
demand justice when red tape and bureaucracy rears
its head, to try to effect improvement.'

Alfie Byrne

In January 1933, Alfie Byrne invited several hundred desti-
tute men and women to an event in the Round Room that
lasted from three in the afternoon 'until late evening'. The
mayor organized a high tea of meat, cakes and fruit, 'and
then gave to every man cigarettes and tobacco and each
woman a box of chocolates'.[1] A few weeks later, he welcomed
Princess Ubangi, a pygmy chieftainess from the Ubangi for-
est in Central Africa, at a reception in the Mansion House.
The *Irish Times* reported, 'Her skin colour is light brown, and
her hair long and straight. She does not speak English, but
laughed a good deal, as if highly pleased with her reception.'[2]
The *Irish Independent* provided more details about the 'viv-
acious copper-coloured lady':

> [She] belongs to a tribe of 250,000 pigmies, is 28 years of
> age, 30 inches tall, and weighs 42 lbs. Her people, said Mr
> J. Gardiner, a New Zealander, who acts as her manager, live
> in trees, have no domestic animals, but kill game for food.

88

The Princess's diet consists of nuts and fruit. She has been
in Europe four months, having just come from Sheffield . . .
The little Princess is at Messrs. Brown Thomas's premises,
Grafton St, Dublin, where she will meet customers daily.
She wears a dress of leopard skin.[3]

That spring, anticipating the local elections in June, the
Lord Mayor distributed a leaflet to householders in his constituency. It included the following words, originally penned
by the American sportswriter Grantland Rice:

> For when the one Great Scorer
> Comes to write against your name
> He writes – not that you won or lost –
> But how you played the game.[4]

Byrne evidently approved of the sentiment, but it was
absurd to claim that winning was irrelevant in a document designed to secure victory. Indeed, the leaflet reveals
his competitive instincts and his interest in new-fangled
marketing methods. He was the first politician to run a
two-colour ad on the front of the *Evening Herald*, he booked
ads on the buses of Dublin, and he gave visitors to the Mansion House a novelty pen or a specially branded box of
chocolates.[5] Design historian Lisa Godson describes the
chocolate box as 'a very clever example of personal brand-
ing and advertisement . . . he was a politician ahead of his
time'.[6]

Byrne was also an early exponent of direct marketing. In
what one paper called 'a master-stroke of electioneering',
Dubliners received what looked like a handwritten letter
from Alfie; in fact, the letters were copies.[7] If a Dubliner
wrote to ask for help ('I have a wife and six children'), he

might be recruited for a few days of work stuffing envelopes.[8] Patrick Byrne recalls:

> Alfie would give out thousands of envelopes to someone who would address the envelopes and they would bring them back a week later. There were certain areas where he was very strong, [like] the North Strand, the East Wall Road, the North Docks. He'd address a personal letter to the woman of the house where there were four or more voters of the same name. And there was a great delivery man who was a pal of his, who'd give Alfie a list of all the breadmen.

Ten days before the council elections, de Valera appealed to voters to put Fianna Fáil candidates on to 'local administrative bodies . . . so that these local bodies could work in conjunction with the Central Government'.[9] The party put up posters claiming that the Lord Mayor had recently visited an event that was boycotted by Catholics. This was a reference to the opening of the Silent Valley waterworks near Belfast, at which Byrne had apparently been 'hobnobbing with Orangemen and Freemasons'.[10] An indignant Lord Mayor led some of his supporters – including his daughter, Mary – to Fianna Fáil headquarters on Amiens Street, where he read aloud telegrams from other Catholics who had attended and approved of the same event. 'I insist on those lying documents in this window being taken down, and not used to deceive the electors,' said Byrne. 'It is a low-down mean misrepresentation, and worthy of the people who put them up.' The *Evening Mail* takes up the story:

> 'Go away,' a voice in the crowd shouted. 'I have men as good as you,' the Lord Mayor retorted, 'and I will not go

away until these lying documents are taken down from the window. While I am in the North Ward no man with guns or batons will frighten me away [cheers]. I say that the people who put these documents are liars, and they must be taken down.'

When a man shouted that the Lord Mayor was inciting a riot, Byrne replied that in Belfast he had made a plea for unity.

A VOICE: You will die very soon.
THE LORD MAYOR: Will you do it?
THE VOICE: I would.
THE LORD MAYOR: Take out your gun now. That is the free-dom these people give others. He says he will make me die. I don't give a snap of my fingers for your threats. If you have a gun produce it now in daylight and not in the dark.
THE VOICE: It is my fists I have.

The tone of the conversation deteriorated further, until there were 'fistic exchanges between members of the crowd, the majority of whom appeared to be supporters of the Lord Mayor'.[11] However, it is unlikely that the fracas had any effect on the result of the election. Once again, Byrne topped the poll. The results in Dublin were disappointing for de Valera; instead of taking control, Fianna Fáil ended up with thirteen seats in a thirty-five-member council. Jim Larkin lost his seat.

In October 1933, the Lord Mayor took part in the Irish National Pilgrimage to Rome. There, he and Seán T. O'Kelly had a private audience with Pope Pius XI. The following day, Byrne and his daughter, Mary, were involved in a car crash, escaping with minor injuries. Because of this accident, they had to stay a few days longer in Rome, and – together with Cissie – they were invited back to the Pope's private library for another audience. This time, Byrne was received as a national figure: 'I want the Irish people and the people of Dublin to know that in receiving you I am receiving them,' the Pope told him.[12]

Byrne clearly made an impression. A few months later it was announced that he would be conferred with the Papal Knighthood of the Grand Cross of the Order of St Sylvester, 'in recognition of Dublin's extensive housing schemes'.[13] A welcome endorsement of his piety and his lobbying for the poor of Dublin, the cross, star and sash of the knighthood became his most treasured possessions. The following year he went on a pilgrimage to Lourdes with 1,300 co-religionists. That autumn, when Byrne's fifth and final son was born, he was christened Sylvester.

The Lord Mayor introduced his son to Dublin at a reception in the Mansion House. Cissie and Alfie were presented with a silver salver and tea service by members of the Corporation and the press. Thanking the guests, Byrne noted that while 'they had not all held the same views on certain matters, those who differed in opinions were either present or had joined in this presentation, which makes me appreciate it all the more'.[14] The chief reporter of the *Irish Times* gushed that Byrne had 'at all times been helpful to the newspaper men'. But of course. The following year, James Joyce would say of Byrne: 'Every day I open the *Irish Times* I see him and his golden chain in some photograph or other.'[15] In the 1930s, amid the rubble of Ascendancy Ireland, editor Bertie Smyllie went looking for new heroes and found Alfie Byrne. In

presenting the office of Lord Mayor as a newsworthy subject, Smyllie conspired in building the legend. However,
Byrne's worldview was sometimes at odds with the Old Lady
of D'Olier Street. He was, for example, a vociferous champion of censorship.

For many years, the Irish state waged a war on films,
books and plays that might corrupt the delicate local mind.
With the establishment of the Film Censorship Office in
1923, the state, in the words of Kevin Rockett, 'took an
extreme, at times an absolutist, if necessarily perversely logic-
al, view of how sexuality, private fantasy and desire should
or, more pertinently, should not be represented'. The first
film censor, James Montgomery, described himself as a
moral sieve whose only principles were the Ten Command-
ments. He once complained about the amount of kissing in
films: 'Why does the cinema lavish miles of celluloid on this
unsanitary salute?'[16]

The state was determined to prevent citizens from being
exposed to offensive films, with the fear of 'imitative action'
informing official policy for many years. In 1932, *Scarface* was
banned for its glamorization of violence. In theory, 'public
opinion' was disgusted by such films, but the popularity of
the cinema suggests otherwise. By the 1950s, Dublin had
more cinema seats per head of population than any other
city in Europe.[17] As we have seen, a younger Byrne had been
involved in an unsuccessful attempt to open a cinema, and as
Lord Mayor he formally opened picture houses on St Stephen's Green and in suburbs such as Fairview, Drumcondra
and Rialto. But a love of cutting ribbons should not be con-
fused with liberality. Byrne supported the Censorship Bill of
1928, the measure that prompted George Bernard Shaw to
warn that the country might slip back into the Atlantic, 'a

little grass patch in which a few million moral cowards are not allowed to call their souls their own by a handful of morbid Catholics'.

Shaw's concern was understandable, but he was wrong about the numbers. It wasn't just a handful of morbid Catholics who supported censorship. Byrne was often petitioned on the subject by anxious constituents. ('For the essence of filth see the *Olympia Review*. I don't want to offend your sense of decency by asking you to see same, but something really ought to be done to censor such filth. It is an outrage to common decency. Sorry to trouble you.')[18] Ever alert to public opinion, Byrne talked up the threat that the arts posed to the delicate Irish psyche. Theatre was a source of particular concern. In 1934, after seeing a 'beautifully clean and educational' production of a play, he sent a warning to other, less reputable outfits:

> We are going to call together the owners of the various theatres and warn them that they must be more careful of the plays they bring before the audiences of Dublin. It is up to them to give us plays such as we have just witnessed . . . If the owners do not listen to our appeal, we shall soon let them see that we mean to take action against them.[19]

After this warning, two officials from Dublin theatres protested their innocence. 'If anything offensive had crept in during the last few weeks, either on the screen or stage, it was unknown to the managers. From now on they would see that nothing offensive would be present.'[20] The *Irish Press* applauded the Lord Mayor for exposing 'a serious evil'. Backing his threat to impose stage censorship, it said the freedom enjoyed by theatre producers was often abused. 'All those connected with the stage should be eager to resist the degradation of an honourable profession by these appeals to the lowest tastes and desires. If, however, reform cannot be secured freely, care for the moral welfare of citizens will demand compulsion.'[21] When a touring company incurred the wrath of the Lord Mayor, the manager assured him that henceforth all of its performers would be 'suitably and decently clad to the satisfaction of the resident manager. Costumes consisting of only trunks and brassieres are not allowed'.[22]

Byrne also endorsed the anti-jazz movement, which was predicated on the fear that dangerous foreign music was infiltrating the dance halls of Ireland; he once assured an audience that 'the citizens of Dublin are not following the dances of negroes'.[23] Of course, the Lord Mayor had no legal authority to do anything about this, and his calls for more censorship met with some ridicule in the press. One journalist observed that the leaders of the purity campaign 'are determined to save the people from themselves'.[24]

On a trip to Glasgow, Byrne became embroiled in a row when he rubbished a speech which claimed that Ireland had made real progress since independence. In reality, he said, unemployment in Dublin had never been so bad. The poor were 'herded like cattle, and have to pay exorbitant rents for rat-infested tenements'. The *Derry Journal* criticized him for speaking so bluntly abroad: 'Instead of taking an Irishman's pride in the speeches of these Scotsmen, Mr Byrne, departing from all established precedent, proceeded to tear Mr Stewart's speech to tatters.'[25]

By January 1935, Byrne was back on message in the *Irish Times*. The Corporation deserved credit, he said, for improving street-lighting, building playgrounds, swimming pools and public baths, and giving the city a new hospital. Half a million pounds would be invested in the water supply. And 2,000 families had been housed in the previous year, with 'an additional 2,000 families in the coming year'. Arguing that money from the Sweepstakes could be used to house the poor of Dublin, there was, he said, 'an urgent demand to house 5,000 families, as some of the old tenements will not last much longer'. The Sweepstakes organizers may have debated Byrne's proposal – the Lord Mayor was a useful ally – but, in the end, they decided to keep building hospitals. Someone else would have to house the poor.

10. Mission to America

In February 1935, James Joyce wrote to his son, Giorgio, 'I see the little Lord Mayor of Dublin Alfie Byrne is going to N.Y.'[1] In fact, Byrne ended up visiting several cities on a much-hyped mission to a country that many an Irishman had tried to conquer, with only mixed success. While the story of the Irish in the United States is often presented as an epic tale of success against the odds, the reality was often far less heroic, and the mid-1930s was a tough time for most Americans, including many with Irish roots.

On 4 March, family and friends – including W. T. Cosgrave – gave Byrne a formal send-off at Dún Laoghaire, as he boarded the mail boat for London en route to New York. He travelled with an agenda: to reach out to the diaspora, promote trade, talk up the Sweepstakes and talk down the border.[2] There was no guarantee that the first Lord Mayor of Dublin to visit North America in forty years would be well received. However, he was in regular contact with the diaspora. In 1931, one Vauleen Alecy wrote from Nashville, Tennessee:

> Possibly you will think this an unusual request but I am writing you to find me a good wife. I want a woman about twenty-five or thirty years old. Must be fairly good looking and a good cook. Anyone you know of have her to write me . . . I have a nice home. All new furniture. I do not drink, have no bad habits.

Byrne sailed from Southampton on the *Olympic*. As he made his way across the Atlantic, the *New York Times* reported that he was 'eager to see this country and to take part in St. Patrick's Parade in New York.' His travelling companion was Peter Trainor Kelly, the head of the Royal Liver's Irish business. The official history of the Royal Liver remembers Kelly as a man 'who created either extreme heat or ice coolness in all his contacts but certainly never lukewarmness'. It is possible that Byrne was double-jobbing on the trip, although to judge from the press coverage it is unlikely that he had much time to devote to company business.

There was a sizeable Irish population in New York, as the local press noted: 'Believe it or not, Alfred Byrne is Lord Mayor of Dublin, but he isn't mayor of the world's largest Irish city. He's visiting it now.'[3] Byrne arrived in the city just in time to celebrate his fifty-third birthday, with 'the self-admitted champion hand-shaker of Europe [receiving] thousands of messages from America and abroad, including a special call from Cardinal Hayes'.[4]

Byrne's teetotalism was a source of bemusement in New York, where the image of the hard-drinking Irishman was well established. On 14 March, the *Evening Mail* reported that he 'came near to forgetting a very important thing to-day. He had been out of bed some hours at the Hotel Astor when he suddenly clapped his traveling comrade, P. T. Kelly, on the back, exclaiming that it is his birthday. Sure enough, Lord Mayor Alfred Byrne is fifty-three today, and he drank to his own good health and long life in (God save us) ginger ale.' When a reporter asked why he wasn't drinking Irish whiskey, Byrne laughed. 'Only ginger ale,' he said, 'that's all I ever take.' Well-wishers flocked to the Byrne suite. 'Those who came were not confined to ginger ale.'[5]

Another paper, the *New York Daily Mirror*, devoted the

whole of its front page to a photograph of Byrne drinking to
the health of New Yorkers on St Patrick's Day. 'The photograph shows the Lord Mayor in the act of putting a foaming
tankard to his lips. It looks remarkably like beer, but the
Lord Mayor's particular vanity is not beer, beer, glorious
beer, but mineral water, as any Dubliner knows.'[6]

The New York Times described Byrne as 'a champion showman' who brought the personal touch to all his campaigns.
'If you ask the poor of North Dublin what they know of
Alfred Byrne they will look at you blankly, but speak of
"Alfie" and you will get some insight into the secret of his
immense personal pull.' Byrne was shadowed by journalists
throughout the trip.[7] When a reporter from the *New York
World Telegram* visited him in his hotel bedroom, he produced
this winning portrait:

> [I found him] twisting his white moustache, a really amazing
> affair with 'sergeant's points' that project approximately one
> full inch from the main body of the moustache. There is a
> convolution in the points and just above the convolution
> they twist upward. The points are waxed and look as sharp
> as a stiletto ... The moustache was really at its best earlier
> today as the Lord Mayor of Dublin twisted it with capable
> fingers as he held court in his suite at the Hotel Astor. And
> the Lord Mayor was at his best, too – a chipper, talkative,
> tiny, temperamental, red-faced gentleman who slaps backs
> resoundingly, pats children on their pates, and is known as
> 'Alfie' by the majority of his admiring constituents.

Throughout the trip Byrne reiterated his claim that the
border was the great deterrent to peace in Ireland. It was
even shoehorned into a message of greeting that was broadcast in cities from New York to Chicago:

In my brief glimpse of America I am convinced there are more Irish in New York than in the whole of Ireland. But the heart of an Irish-man is always true to the Ould Sod. That's why we'll be seeing shamrocks on a million American lapels tomorrow. Conditions in Ireland are like those in every other country in the world, suffering from the world-wide depression. But I think the peak point of the depression has passed, and we are on the return journey to prosperity. Ireland suffers from a world-wide complaint in that her young men and women are leaving the land to come to towns and cities, there to be disappointed by failure to find suitable employment, and thus placing a heavy burden on the public authorities who must care for them. However, a number of small industries are growing up behind the tariff walls in Ireland's towns and cities. The boundary question between the north and south of Ireland is still a barrier to peace, progress and happiness among our people. While that boundary exists there will be trouble among my countrymen.[8]

It is in New York that one of the most enduring 'Alfie' myths has its roots. After seeing Mae West perform on Broadway, Byrne allegedly visited the star in her dressing room. Charmed by the Irishman, Miss West is said to have used her catchphrase, 'Come up and see me sometime.'

The Lord Mayor blushed before stuttering, 'I c-c-can't.'

'Why not?' said West.

'Because it's Lent,' replied Byrne.

'Well, in that case,' she snapped, 'come up and see me when you get it back.'

Byrne's obsession with censorship and his paranoid view of cinema were both evident on the day he visited the headquarters of the New York Police Department. While praising the police

for their efficiency, he bemoaned 'the city's leniency in permit-
ting moving pictures of criminal activity'. His concern was raised
after seeing a line-up in which the usual suspects evidently
resembled Edward G. Robinson and James Cagney. 'He didn't
approve of the jauntiness of many of the suspected gunmen and
burglars in the line-up. They looked like exhibitionists, he said.
He blamed the movies for glorifying the criminal.'[9]

On the same trip, Byrne was formally conferred with the
Freedom of Toronto.[10] And in Boston, he found himself at a
loss for words – a rare occurrence – when he was given an
official greeting in Irish, and couldn't understand it. Anxious
to avoid embarrassment, he assured reporters that his children were 'now learning Gaelic at schools'.[11] The incident
happened at a lunch for hundreds of Irish-Americans, where
Byrne was the guest of honour. The Mayor of Boston
reminded his audience that there were as many people of
Irish blood in Boston as there were in Dublin. When Byrne
urged them to buy more Irish goods, a prominent Boston
merchant pointed out that Irish producers should pay more
attention 'to the needs of the American buying public'. Byrne
replied with a tirade about the high quality of Irish tweeds,
woollens, linens, whiskeys and beer. Still, the luncheon
ended in good spirits, with a former Mayor of Boston, John
Fitzgerald, singing 'The Wearin' of the Green'.[12]

In Washington D.C., Byrne made a visit to the White
House to pay his respects to President Roosevelt. It was on
this leg of the trip that the Lord Mayor became the victim of
a burglary. The unfortunate incident made the headlines in
many newspapers:

Ald. Byrne, Lord Mayor of Dublin, [was robbed] of his most
treasured possessions – gold and diamond ornaments and the

Cross, Star and Sash of the Knighthood of St. Sylvester, which was conferred on him by the Pope. All mysteriously disappeared while Ald. Byrne was visiting Washington. The loss was discovered last Friday after a large crowd of important personages had been visiting him in his suite at the Mayflower Hotel. The robbery was not revealed, however, until yesterday. The intrinsic value of the articles stolen is given as £2,000. Ald. Byrne is stated to be very much upset by his loss.[13]

Suspicion fell on the grandees who had visited the Lord Mayor in his suite, but eventually Byrne admitted, 'I mislaid them myself in Washington, and no one else is to blame.' He was, he said, 'confident that when they are found, and the finder realizes what they are, they will be returned to me'. But didn't the newspapers say the articles were worth a fortune? Apparently, that was a mistake. 'They are not of great intrinsic value,' Byrne insisted, 'but sentimentally they are priceless.'[14]

The American talk-show host David Letterman once said of a politician, 'The Senator got so tired on the campaign trail that he started kissing hands and shaking babies.' Towards the end of his American trip, pressmen were surprised to see Byrne using only his left hand. Meeting thousands of New Yorkers 'had left his right hand temporarily useless'.[15] When he was photographed in repose for the *New York Daily Mirror*, the caption read: 'The Lord Mayor, known as Europe's champion handshaker, was snapped in an "off moment". He isn't shaking hands.'[16]

Despite the heartache of losing his Papal garb and the gruelling itinerary, the trip was a success, enhancing the reputation of the Free State, bringing it closer to America and promoting the legend of Alfie Byrne. The pint-sized mayor had generated column inches for over twenty years, but now he was playing on a larger stage and, in the process, he was promoting Ireland as a destination long before the state got around to marketing itself.

For the rest of his life, Byrne fielded tourism-related enquiries. That summer, a Dubliner sent him a 'Come to Ireland' song. A man from Indiana asked where to buy a genuine Irish shillelagh. And the Lord Mayor continued to talk up Ireland overseas. On one occasion, he told an English audience, 'We have a beautiful little country, with splendid golf, the best fishing and hunting, and perhaps – now don't misunderstand me – may I say shooting too?'[17]

Byrne's pioneering work was eventually recognized by the State when the new tourism board asked if they could use his name and image to sell Ireland abroad: 'Your name and your photograph are familiar to the readers of newspapers in a number of American cities.'[18] The Lord Mayor enjoyed his role as national barker and was happy to oblige. He never stopped sharing information with curious visitors, many of them Americans impressed by his showmanship in the spring of 1935. Eighty years later, tourism is the largest indigenous industry on the island of Ireland.[19]

In the summer of 1935, Byrne was re-elected as Lord Mayor for a sixth consecutive year, again defeating Kathleen Clarke. He won, as always, with a shopping list of endorsements and promises. In newspaper advertisements, he published the names of Fine Gael and independent councillors on the 'Lord Mayor's Panel'. These erstwhile allies kept the archschemer in power. On this occasion, the result was greeted with loud applause and, over the next few days, newspapers printed tributes in verse.

CONGRATULATIONS to you, my Lord Mayor!
For the sixth time you will fill the mayoral chair
Where for five years you've set a furious pace.

As the first citizen of Dublin Town
We hail you once again – long may you reign.
We know that you will never let us down
While on your shoulders hangs the Mayoral chain.[20]

One Sunday morning shortly after the election, when O'Connell Street looked particularly shabby, Byrne invited the *Evening Herald* to witness 'the promiscuous scattering of the litter in the form of papers, empty cigarette and match boxes'. There can be little doubt about the provenance of the report that, 'at his own expense, [the Lord Mayor] engaged the services of a number of young people to collect the litter and deposit it in the receptacles provided for it'.[21] A few weeks later, Byrne lamented the 'thoughtless evil' of people who break bottles and leave the pieces lying in places where they can do damage. 'Undoubtedly, carelessness is one of the commonest ills from which the human race suffers, and it is a very troublesome and costly one.'[22]

That September, Byrne presented the painter Sir John Lavery with the Freedom of Dublin. Guests at the ceremony included John McCormack, Seán T. O'Kelly and W. T. Cosgrave. 'In days of anxiety and tribulation,' said Byrne, 'this country had faithful and loyal adherents in the Lavery household in London.'[23] When the Lord Mayor recalled Lady Lavery's death and her love of Ireland, 'tears were seen on the distinguished painter's cheeks'.[24] Invited to speak, Lavery struggled to his feet. 'You understand,' he said, 'that on occasions like this words are very hard to find to express one's feelings.' But then he remembered a winning anecdote.

My first effort to unite paint and politics had been to invite Sir Edward Carson and the late Mr John Redmond to sit for me, the condition being that the portraits would be placed side by side in the National Gallery of Dublin. I considered Sir Edward Carson the better subject for a painter, but when Carson saw the portrait he said: 'Well, it is easy to see which side you are on.' When Redmond saw the portraits he said: 'Well, I always had an idea that Carson and I might be hanging together in Dublin one day, and it has come to pass.'

Lavery said his wife 'insisted it was my duty as an Irishman to do something for my country. The collection now in your gallery is the result.' Pausing, he said, 'My feelings are so intense that I cannot go on.' Then he sat down. It was a poignant moment in the life of a painter who was already a member of the academies of Rome, Paris, Berlin, Antwerp, Milan, Brussels and Stockholm. Today he is remembered as a good husband, a fine artist and a Freeman of Dublin.

The Freedom of Dublin is still offered to distinguished individuals, and the mayor continues to bestow the honour. At the time of writing, there are eighty-one members of the club. They include Charles Stewart Parnell, John Redmond, Douglas Hyde, John McCormack, Lorenzo Lauri, George Bernard Shaw, Seán T. O'Kelly, Éamon de Valera and Maureen Potter. We do not know if Alfie Byrne would have accepted the Freedom of Dublin, because he was never invited to do so.

It was one of the prizes that remained beyond his reach.

11. The Shaking Hand of Dublin

'For God's sake! Could you find me any
post at all? I am absolutely distracted. I hope you will
forgive me for troubling you. I know you will
and I certainly will never forget it to you.'
Undated letter to Byrne from a man
living on South Anne Street

The subject of this book made his name as a politician in a
sleepy part of a fading empire, and even when his home town
became the capital of an independent nation, the Lord Mayor
of Dublin had little real power. A former occupant of that
distinguished office once told this author, 'Councillors are
the lowest form of political life. Even at the top, you're still a
bottom-feeder.' But perception is everything in politics, and
Alfie Byrne had a master's degree in smoke and mirrors.
Consider the following by Denis Gwynn, from the *Cork
Examiner* in 1963:

> He would deliberately drive his car slowly through a crowded
> street in some poor district until he saw a shabby boy's bi-
> cycle parked against the pavement. He would then carefully
> drive close to it until he knocked it over. There would be
> cries of distress all round. Alfie Byrne would then leap from
> his own car, with every sign of acute regret and ask who was
> the unfortunate owner of the old bicycle. A messenger boy

would be brought forward, and Alfie would express his utter dismay at what he had done. He would at once insist that the boy must have a new bicycle at his expense and that he would apologise in person to his parents. A crowd would form quickly and Alfie Byrne's familiar kindly face would be recognised at once. He would buy the new bicycle there and then; and the story would spread far and wide in a district where he was already regarded as a most generous servant of the people.[1]

Byrne claimed no acts of statesmanship: 'these are for more able than I'. Instead, his concern was 'bread and butter' issues. In a piece of election literature from the 1940s, he listed them: 'housing and old-age pensions; a cut in relief to be investigated; a house condemned, an area flooded, accommodation wanted; hospital or sanatorium accommodation needed; a business man in difficulty; a National Health benefit disputed'. In the 1930s, as the economy continued to falter and thousands of Dubliners emigrated to England, this is the sort of question he was asked all the time: 'I am very sorry to tell you that I am still out of work and there does not seem any prospects of work but I wish to know if you could possibly lend me a pound to buy old scrap iron?'[2] If the journalist who claimed that Byrne would leave a banquet to answer a call from the poorest woman in Dublin was exaggerating, it was only slightly. And there were many such calls:

> Every day, people write him between 50 and 80 letters, asking him to arrange a new house or to help them redeem pawned blankets or get the ex-school-boy a job, or prevent an eviction, or get a bed in a hospital, even to settle a dispute with a mother-in-law or have the landlord gaoled, and

Alfie reads each single letter himself, dictates replies, arranges whatever help he can quietly.[3]

Most of those letters were, of course, from constituents – but in many cases, Byrne had nothing to gain from his own generosity. In the autumn of 1935, a woman arrived in Dublin from New Zealand with five children in tow. While she was in the city, her father died and her husband lost his job in Auckland. The woman had become liable to pay rates; Byrne offered to give her fifty pounds if the Board of Assistance subscribed the same sum to pay her fare home, but another member of the board objected, saying it 'should not allow the Lord Mayor to fleece himself'. The board refused to countenance spending ratepayers' money, and the proposal was defeated.[4]

Byrne was a stranger to relaxation. His appointments diary reads like an inventory of Dublin landmarks ('8pm Jammets. 9pm Switzers Staff Dance at the Metropole'[5]) and he regularly attended a dozen events in a single day. There were many short speeches, and while he seldom said witty things, his grandiloquent orations had a roundabout charm. There was the time, for example, when he presented the prizes at a southside tennis club. Noting that he seldom saw the same lady champions two years in a row, Byrne observed that tennis 'was first played in the parks of French chateaux in the middle ages. Is it an arena for the courts of love and the permanent partnership of two contestants? If so, confirmed bachelors should keep away from tennis clubs.'[6]

In September 1935, the Minister for Industry, Seán Lemass, presided at the opening of the Theatre Royal. Byrne was there in his top hat and morning suit, a costume bound to irritate any Fianna Fáil politician. With 3,850 seats in a single auditorium, an electric Compton organ and its own troupe of dancers, the Royal hosted stars like Jimmy Cagney, Nat King Cole and Bob Hope. Judy Garland thrilled two thousand Dubliners who couldn't get tickets to her concert by singing from her dressing-room window. And Danny Kaye was fondly remembered by taxi drivers for many years, because he sang so many encores that everyone missed the last bus home. Despite his oft-repeated concern about 'films of harmful character', Byrne was happy to revel in the success of the Royal, because it was a good-news story for Dublin.

That November, Byrne presided at the opening of the Mount Street Club for the Unemployed. The club was financed through a public appeal for donations, and everything from the plumbing to the decoration of the building was supplied gratis by local tradesmen. A barter system was established in which every member had to give two hours' labour a week. The *Belfast Newsletter* explained the system: 'If a man wants a meal he will pay for it with a "tally", which is equivalent to an hour's work. He can obtain a haircut, a bath, a game of billiards, clothes, material to mend his furniture, his boots, and his bicycle all in exchange for a certain number of "tallys".'[7]

Later that month, a journalist from the *Sunday Dispatch* reported:

> I called on Lord Mayor Alfie Byrne, and I found him sitting at a desk which was littered with pawn-tickets. The tickets were not the Lord Mayor's own. Their presence on his desk was largely due to the miserable weather. Among the scattered pile were tickets for a pair of blankets pawned for 4s.,

for a little boy's overcoat pawned for 2s., and for a pair of child's shoes pawned for 9d.; and they were there because their owners, all in dire need, had appealed to the Lord Mayor to redeem them. Such expenditure can only be met out of the Lord Mayor's own pocket; but though he well knew demands would increase a hundredfold between now and Christmas, he was trying to meet them all. And there are still people who believe that a Lord Mayor has a fine soft job and a big fat salary.[8]

That winter, the poor of Dublin were, as usual, struggling to pay for necessities. At a meeting of the Mansion House Coal Fund, Byrne said the committee 'had been compelled to restrict its activities, owing to the high cost of coal [because of the Economic War] and a reduction in the total of subscriptions as compared with previous years'.[9] Byrne pleaded with the public to come to such meetings, so that 'they could learn at first-hand what is being done'. He made an earnest plea for help. Such representations made for good theatre, and like any actor, Byrne appreciated a large audience. Hence the offer of a seat in the stalls.

That December, Seán Lemass formally opened a new factory in Bray. Ribbon-cutting is a pretext for back-slapping, that most congenial of political exercises, but Byrne was not in a flexible mood. Lemass spoke at great length; when a crony followed him with a speech on the wit and wisdom of Seán Lemass, Byrne stood up, shouted 'Question!', and lambasted Lemass for his 'rather boastful and dangerous lecture'.[10] (In fact, Lemass made a relatively innocuous speech, although Byrne may have felt slighted by some breach of protocol.)

Most people went to Bray for the beach. The Lord Mayor

went for the scuffle. There is something complex and interesting about *that* Alfie Byrne, but in the press he was fast becoming the caricature that would later render him of little interest to serious historians. As a glowing report in the *Sunday Chronicle* once put it, 'His good works are never denied and rarely decried, even by his enemies.' The same journalist claimed that 'the energetic, able Alfie [is so popular] that he has to go about some of his work by night so as to avoid notice'. According to this legend, when a policeman discovered the mayor 'clambering over some old ruins', Byrne revealed his plan 'for giving Christmastide relief jobs to the workless in removing derelict dwellings. He was going around to note the extent of the work involved at that hour because by day he was sure to meet so many people who knew him.'[11] This image, of a leader so popular that he had to do reconnaissance work in the dead of night, is unfamiliar to a generation that regards politics as a field in which crooks flourish in broad daylight!

When the journalist Con O'Leary visited the official residence, the Lord Mayor kept being called away to conferences of mercy: 'One must be prepared for all sorts of interruption, for he is pre-eminently the friend and counsellor of the poor, who approach him on various missions.'[12] Another reporter who called to the Mansion House found Byrne absent: 'He had gone to an eviction in the heart of the city. His mission was to call off the bailiffs on behalf of a poor woman.'[13]

Byrne's devotion to the job was at least once the cause of a domestic misunderstanding. In January 1939, the *Daily Sketch* reported:

His day begins about ten in the morning, and frequently continues until the small hours of the following morning, for he places himself at the disposal of citizens of all creeds and classes. He told me of one occasion when he arrived home tired and hungry after everybody had gone to bed, and had to explore the basement of the Mansion House himself in search of food, eventually dining off two cold cooked sausages, a crust of bread, and a glass of milk. Next morning he found the family discussing the burglars who had broken in during the night and ransacked the basement.

Again, it is worth reminding ourselves that hyperbole unites so many of these stories. This is what happens when a master salesman spends years planting legends in the press. However, Byrne also built an electoral machine against formidable odds, largely on the back of his personal appeal, and by the mid-1930s, *everyone* was on first-name terms with Alfie. That was no small achievement. The Shaking Hand of Dublin told a good story about empowering citizens at every level of Irish society, but he was also a serious political operator, with powerful enemies in the Fianna Fáil government. He was sharp because he had to be.

In December 1932, an editorial in the *Evening Herald* claimed, 'Dublin is faced with a winter of dire distress. Evictions by the hundred are threatened.'[14] The Lord Mayor pleaded for a moratorium on outstanding arrears for Corporation tenants, 'because eviction will mean death to many'. As we have seen, Byrne once highlighted the plight of two families – a total of sixteen people – who were forced to share one room. Working alongside political rivals such as Jim Larkin and Tom Kelly, he spent most of his adult life trying to help people who were scared of the future.

Byrne was firmly committed to big government. 'The

economists who preach saving in this country are all wrong,'
he said. 'Such propaganda is harming the country. Now is
the time for every Council, County Council, Corporation
and other public body with spending powers to be instructed
to put in hand, without delay, any works that they may have
been considering.'[15]

Fianna Fáil is often credited for its work in the provision
of public housing during the 1930s. But it was the Housing
(Miscellaneous Provisions) Act in 1931, the year before
Fianna Fáil came to power, that first gave the state some of
the necessary muscle. Providing for the appointment of a
new housing architect for Dublin Corporation, the Act
increased powers to identify appropriate sites and make
Compulsory Purchase Orders (CPO). This would transform
the relationship between the state, landowners and Dublin's
poor – and not always for the good.

Major new public housing schemes were built in Marino,
Drumcondra and Crumlin, to house the slum-dwellers of
Dublin. When the first new residents arrived out to Crumlin, the only civic amenity in place was a 900-seat Catholic
church. Two years later, the children of the area still had to
travel back to their old schools in town, because the new
ones were not yet built.[16] The war on slums was all very well,
but the rent in the new 'estates was higher, the tram fares
were crippling, and for casual labourers there was no guarantee of work once they made it into town'.[17] As a result,
many Dubliners resented moving.

Crucially, however, the Church supported the development of new suburbs in the Garden City style that was
fashionable in England at the time. Diarmaid Ferriter has
observed that Fianna Fáil ministers sometimes boasted that
'their policies were in line with Catholic social teaching as

endorsed by the Vatican'. Inspired by the superstition that 'people who live at lower density have higher morals', senior clerics worked with planning officials to ensure that churches and schools secured prominent positions at the centre of the new suburbs, where it would, of course, be easier to minister to the flock.[18]

On the subject of housing, Byrne found himself at odds with the general trend. He wanted to rebuild the inner core rather than erect new homes on the outskirts of the city. In 1935, he told an audience in Leeds: 'Public authorities ought to hesitate about, and go slow in, sending out any distance the working-class population, whose work is in the heart of the city.'[19] And here he is in Liverpool two years later: 'The demolition of your tenements, and the erection of these splendid flats in the centre of your city – near the people's work – is a model of perfection which other great cities should try to emulate.'[20]

Byrne wanted a proper system of self-contained flats at reasonable rents in the heart of the city. It was another half-won battle. Between 1932 and 1939, Dublin Corporation designed and built 7,638 dwellings. Of those, 1,002 were flats. Despite the fact that it was cheaper for a family to rent a flat, the Corporation preferred what the architectural historian Ellen Rowley has called the tabula rasa of new estates: 'This viewpoint was rooted in the largely middle-class reformers' disgust and, in turn, fear of slum squalor.'[21]

There were some tangible successes, and Byrne was quick, as ever, to take credit. Interviewed by the *Sunday Times* in 1935, he offered to demonstrate how the council was building decent housing. 'So off we went to the site of the old D'Arcy Brewery between the quays and Thomas Street, where flats to house 300 families are in course of erection. When the car drew up it was soon surrounded by crowds of cheering youngsters, all of whom knew their friend, "Mr Alfie".[22]

When Byrne led a delegation from the Housing Committee to inspect the new Oliver Bond Complex, 315 families were housed there. Much of it was commissioned by Herbert Simms, an Englishman who personally signed off the drawings for seventeen thousand new homes during his time working for Dublin Corporation.

The old Corporation was suspended, at least in part, because of corruption in the provision of housing. As Byrne was a member of the powerful housing sub-committee in the new Corporation for many years, it was perhaps inevitable that someone would accuse him of foul play. In 1938, the Minister for Finance, Seán MacEntee, said Byrne was abusing his position by interfering in the allocation of housing 'irrespective of the merits of each case'. Byrne denied the charge, pointing out that MacEntee's Fianna Fáil colleague Tom Kelly was chairman of the Housing Committee, 'thus responsible for any decisions made'. Besides, the granting of houses was dealt with by the city manager, P. J. Hernon, and his team in the Housing Department, 'based upon plans laid down' by the Housing Committee 'and approved by Mr MacEntee's friends in the Government'.[23]

Did the Lord Mayor protest too much? In Bill Cullen's memoir *It's a Long Way from Penny Apples*, we learn that the businessman's father worked for the Lord Mayor during the Eucharistic Congress. Byrne provided him with the reference that led to a job in a timber merchant's. Sixteen years later, Bill Cullen went to see Byrne. This time, he wanted help getting out of the slums. 'Six kids, Billy,' said Byrne, 'and you and Mary still in one room in Summerhill. I can't believe it.' Apparently, Byrne said: 'Those Summerhill tenements will be knocked down, if it's the last thing I do on this earth. We've new houses being built in Donnycarney and Crumlin and Ballyfermot and I'll make sure your name goes top of the list.'

A few days later, Bill Cullen writes, Byrne came to Summerhill in his black Renault Vivastella. Getting out of the car, he was swamped by black-shawled women and children. Audience at the ready, Byrne said that he had come to give the entire street some good news. 'Dublin Corporation have made the decision to demolish the whole of these tenements in Summerhill within the next twelve months, and there's a new house for every family.'

Bill Cullen has admitted fusing memory and imagination in the writing of his memoir. This is what he has Alfie Byrne saying to the Cullen family as he finished a bowl of coddle in their tenement room that day:

> So I have to head off now but let me tell you that Billy Cullen's name is top of the list in the Corporation for rehousing. You'll probably get a choice of Ballyfermot or Donnycarney, but just head over to the Housing Office on Tuesday at ten o'clock and ask for John Hogan. He's my man and he'll take care of you.[24]

The Cullens were offered a house in Ballyfermot: 'the empty fields of culchie land'. They could not afford to move out there, so John Hogan offered them Donnycarney. That was too far away from their stall on Henry Street. Eventually, Hogan found a two-bedroom apartment for them in Portland Row in the inner city: 'In fact, there's a choice of two in houses we've just renovated.'

Even allowing for exaggeration in Cullen's account, it is clear that the mayor lobbied officials on behalf of

Alfred Byrne MP shortly after his election to Westminster in 1915. At thirty-three, Byrne was one of the youngest MPs in the Irish Party. The oldest, Samuel Young, was ninety-four. Byrne soon fell for the rituals and pageantry of Westminster: the morning suits, the top hats, the arcane procedures and the lavish surroundings.

Cissie Heagney married Byrne in 1910. Her father, Tom Heagney, was Byrne's boss, a cute country publican of a type still prominent in Dublin today. Cissie gave birth to ten children, of whom eight survived to adulthood. She often took the children on holiday without their father.

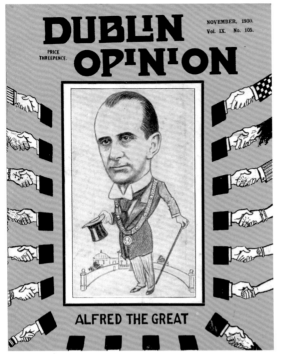

DUBLIN OPINION

PRICE
THREEPENCE.

NOVEMBER, 1930.
Vol. IX. No. 105.

ALFRED THE GREAT

In the first of seven appearances on the cover of *Dublin Opinion*, Byrne had no facial hair. Making a return in January 1931, the twiddly moustache distracted attention from the poor condition of his front teeth. The teeth were upgraded in 1934, but he kept the facial hair until the very end.

Byrne welcomes Cardinal Lorenzo Lauri, the Papal Legate, to the Eucharistic Congress in Dublin on 20 June 1932. 'May I be permitted, as Lord Mayor of Dublin, officially to express something of the sentiments that fill every heart today towards the august person of Your Eminence.'

Watched by the former president of the Executive Council W. T. Cosgrave and Lord Mayor Alfie Byrne, Fine Gael president Eoin O'Duffy takes the salute at a rally at the Mansion House in 1934. Byrne had supported the merger between Cosgrave's party and O'Duffy's Blueshirts. (*Irish Times*)

THE LORD MAYOR LEAVES NEW YORK.

Alfie Byrne's handshake was a gift for local comedians. After his visit to North America in 1935, a cartoon in *Dublin Opinion* depicted the Lord Mayor walking up the gangplank of a ship. His many well-wishers all have their right hand bandaged in a sling. Note the cat, perched on a rooftop, with one paw in a sling.

Byrne with his son Louis Sylvester on Dún Laoghaire pier in the summer of 1936. When Byrne got into the habit of boarding mail boats to welcome distinguished visitors to Dún Laoghaire, a Fianna Fáil councillor complained that the Lord Mayor 'comes out here to usurp our chairman's functions'.

Byrne in conversation with Fine Gael politicians Desmond FitzGerald, Patrick McGilligan and W. T. Cosgrave in 1934. Byrne had recently been conferred with the Papal Knighthood of the Grand Cross of the Order of St Sylvester. The cross, star and sash of the knighthood soon became his most treasured possessions.

For several months leading up to the coronation of King George VI in May 1937, there was intense speculation as to whether Byrne would go to London for the festivities. On 27 April, the Lord Mayor received a politely worded threat.

Shortly before Dr Douglas Hyde was inaugurated as the first president of Ireland in 1938, he accepted an invitation to pose outside Leinster House. The Lord Mayor looks comfortable beside Dr Hyde, but this was grace under pressure, for a strange combination of forces had just colluded to deprive Byrne of a crowning honour. (National Library of Ireland)

On 27 June 1939, Kathleen Clarke's first act as Lord Mayor of Dublin was to tell Alfie Byrne that she would not wear the mayoral chain that had been presented to the city by King William of Orange. 'I will take the smaller chain instead.' The figure on the left of the picture is Alderman Tom Kelly.

DUBLIN OPINION

July, 1939
Price Threepence.

The National Humorous Journal of Ireland.

Alfie atque Vale.

'Hail and farewell Alfie.' In the summer of 1939, *Dublin Opinion* marked the end of Byrne's reign with a whimsical salute to the eternal hand-shaker. Byrne soon faced what a dramatist would call his central crisis. Who was he, if *not* the Lord Mayor of Dublin?

Byrne left school at the age of thirteen to work as a mechanic in a bicycle shop at the bottom of Dawson Street. He cycled the streets of Dublin for over fifty years, and prided himself on the fact that he always carried out running repairs on his own bicycle.

Byrne with his sons Tom and Louis on the steps of Leinster House in November 1952, after Tom's election as a TD. Another son, Alfie Jr, had died at the age of thirty-nine, prompting a by-election in Dublin North-west.

Byrne in 1955, during his tenth and final term as Lord Mayor. Enlarging the office of mayor, he made Dublin a source of pride all over the country. In the press, he was known as the Lord Mayor of Ireland.

The funeral of Alfie Byrne leaves the Pro-Cathedral for Glasnevin cemetery. (*Irish Independent*/Getty Images)

constituents. We also know that he received thousands of begging letters. ('My wife is expecting a baby in February and I have five small children as well . . . I live in a small top front room and the rain comes in.')[25] We do not know if he privileged constituents 'irrespective of the merits of each case'. Nor do we know what he did to try to influence officials.

Byrne certainly kept people abreast of good news, often before it became official. But that was standard practice. It was so common that the Corporation printed form letters that began with the words 'With reference to _____ representations regarding your need for rehousing . . .' A copy of the letter was sent to the member in question and, in that way, something was seen to be done. In addition, Byrne also printed form letters for tenants in trouble. They only required a name and the Lord Mayor's signature:

> *Dear _____, I attended the Corporation Housing Committee meeting a few days ago and regret to say your name was on a list of proposed ejectments for rent arrears.*
>
> *Do please hurry and make the best offer you can, with a payment weekly off the balance. Call to Rents Revenue Department and ask for Mr Codd the Officer in Charge of Rents Department. You will find him reasonable and fair, but you must act quickly.*

Sometimes there were squabbles with officials. In January 1936, after yet more flooding, tenants from Coady's Cottages in the North Strand, which were officially condemned as unfit for habitation, reminded the Lord Mayor that the Corporation was about to take possession of twenty-eight new houses nearby. Could they have them? The *Evening Herald* said Byrne was sympathetic, calling for a special meeting of the Housing Committee as soon as possible, 'at which he would put forward their request'. This grandstanding was not appreciated in City Hall. A few days later, the *Irish Times* revealed that the city manager and the Lord Mayor had suffered their first 'difference of opinion . . . in their association of more than five years'. Most of the time, Hernon and Byrne were collaborators who would lunch together in the Dolphin Hotel.

That winter the council accepted a loan of £250,000 from the Royal Liver to fund public housing. Byrne arranged the loan and was formally thanked by the Corporation. The *Irish Times* reported that he managed to save his local government £5,000, 'which would have been the cost if the loan had been promoted in the ordinary way'.[26] As we have seen, Byrne was praised for facilitating this and other loans to public bodies all over the country. There were few if any complaints about conflicts of interest. Only once, back in 1927, a journalist noted that the Royal Liver 'has the right of nomination of tenants'.[27] Did Byrne enjoy these special powers? And for how long? Was this why people said Alfie Byrne could fix that for you? Or was that just a myth?

These questions are complicated by the fact that politicians routinely overstate their influence. By 1939, the Lord Mayor was claiming that the Corporation had cleared many of the slum areas on his watch. 'People who visited Dublin twenty years ago returning now would hardly recognize it as the same city.'[28] But conditions still remained grim for many Dubliners – a few days later, Byrne was comforting residents after the roof of their tenement house collapsed – and the Corporation, hampered by a lack of funding and real autonomy, struggled to cope with demand. In 1948, an official rejected one of Byrne's appeals for help with the words:

Mrs Buckley's family consists of eight persons in one room and she has not been housed yet for the reason that there were larger families living in one room and other more urgent clearance cases who had to be housed before her. She will be notified in due course when her case is reached.[29]

12. The Empire Mind and the Orchard Thieves

Alfie Byrne's view of Britain was both hopelessly outdated and way ahead of its time. He told voters, 'I believe in friendly relations with Great Britain and Northern Ireland and the Commonwealth, and I have always striven for this.'[1] A constitutional nationalist who opposed the border with Northern Ireland, he relished his time in the House of Commons, where he honed his conception of Irish patriotism without wishing to leave the Commonwealth. He did not like violence. And he did like the English: their manners, their rituals, their pageantry – further, they paid him good money as a trustee for the Royal Liver. All this made him a target for nationalist abuse.

When Éamon de Valera started a trade war with Ireland's largest trading partner, Byrne lamented this petty act of self-harm. In fact, he opposed de Valera on most aspects of the Anglo-Irish relationship. The two men did, however, agree on one thing: Ireland should be united. And how might that happen? Byrne thought that if everyone was nicer to each other, Ireland could be reconciled to itself. 'I am convinced that a United Ireland can only be achieved by goodwill, good government, toleration, and respect for each other's views, political aims and business ambitions – it's my way to unite Ireland.'[2]

John Bowman has observed that one of the recurrent themes in modern Irish history is 'the widespread naivety or self-deception that often led Irish nationalists to play the Catholic card while simultaneously preaching the virtues of a united Ireland'.[3] Byrne was an early exponent of such magical thinking. Allowing that there was 'misunderstanding' between the British and Irish Governments, this loyal Catholic spent thirty years arguing that the real problem was the border between northern and southern Ireland, and that Ireland was too small for two parliaments.[4]

After independence, many people said the figure on top of the Nelson Pillar should be replaced with someone acceptable to nationalists, such as Patrick Pearse. When some colleagues on the City Council called for the pillar to be removed altogether, Byrne demurred. Trade in O'Connell Street might suffer, he said, if the old landmark was taken down, as it was 'a point to which the public come from all parts. The Pillar plays the part of a safety valve for traffic, both vehicular and pedestrian.'[5] Byrne was being cute in pointedly ignoring all that historical baggage, but he had his reasons. He knew that many Dubs saw the pillar as an integral part of the city, and Nelson was a proper hero as well as a popular presence. When a constituent wrote to ask if Byrne had the power to replace Nelson with the Blessed Virgin, the Lord Mayor had one of his secretaries reply: 'I am directed by the Lord Mayor to thank you for your letter with reference to Nelson Pillar and to say that the matter comes before the Corporation regularly. Your proposal will have his consideration when the matter arises again.'[6]

In October 1935, Byrne attended a lunch in the Garrick Theatre in London. It was the first time in forty years that the Lord Mayors of London and Dublin had met. A few months later, Byrne further alienated the Irish government by attending a pontifical high Mass at Westminster Cathedral in memory of the late King George V. He was the only Irish representative at the event, apart from a minor civil servant, and his presence was a subterfuge, using Catholic worship as cover for Anglophilia.

Byrne had met the king during his time as an MP.[7] His decision to attend the memorial Mass was, he said, 'an act that the vast majority of the Irish people would endorse'. Elsewhere he characterized it as 'nothing but a simple duty that the citizens of Dublin would expect of me that I should pay due respect on their behalf'.[8] Critics interpreted de Valera's refusal to send a representative as a petty gesture. Through his presence at the funeral, where he was seated with the Lord Mayors of London and Edinburgh, Byrne was deliberately endorsing a broader understanding of what it meant to be Irish: tolerant, compassionate and prepared to make peace. It was a magnanimous act, but his attendance would have repercussions. In fact, he was castigated even before his return to Dublin.

Two days later, in Liverpool City Council Chambers, a Reverend Longbottom objected to the presence of Byrne: 'He does not belong to our Empire, and we do not want Sinn Féiners here. Send Paddy back to Ireland.' When order had been restored, the Lord Mayor of Dublin turned to the Lord Mayor of Liverpool. 'I thank you sincerely,' he said, 'for the kind invitation of your members and their kind reception.'[9]

Byrne's appearance at the royal Mass was reheated in the local election campaign of 1936, when he was accused of holding a 'commonwealth outlook'.[10] Responding to the charge, Byrne demanded to know 'what action, words or deeds of mine or any of my colleagues, at any time, misrepresented this country . . . It is grossly unfair for any citizen to stand on a public platform and make misleading statements with reference to the valuable work done by public representatives in the interests of the people.'[11]

*

Under new rules enacted by the Minister for Local Government, Seán T. O'Kelly, the universal franchise was introduced for local elections in 1936, doubling the size of the City Council electorate. The rules of the system were about to change, and pressmen speculated that Byrne might be one of the victims of the new dispensation. When Seán Lemass said the capital of a country with a Fianna Fáil government should have a Fianna Fáil mayor, the *Irish Times* offered this bullish defence of its man in the Mansion House:

> Alderman Byrne has preserved a sturdy independence which has won him golden opinions in all quarters. He never has forgotten the fact that, as Lord Mayor, he is the representative, not of a class, a creed or a party but of all the citizens of Ireland's ancient capital. His capacity for hard work is almost incredible, and his popularity is without parallel in the annals of our city. We are convinced that no other man in Ireland to-day can replace Alderman Byrne as Lord Mayor. For that reason we regret very much that Mr Lemass should declare publicly that a member of the Fianna Fáil party ought to be chosen.[12]

The election results were a triumph for Byrne. Out of a poll of 137,749, a total of 72,658 votes – over 52 per cent – were cast for the Lord Mayor's Panel, the 28 candidates who ran with his support. Byrne personally polled 14,297 first preferences: at least double the vote of every other candidate but one. The *Evening Mail* said his personality 'has dominated the campaign', and described the election as 'a remarkable personal triumph for the Lord Mayor'. The decision to give his blessing to named Fine Gael and Independent candidates was cited as a factor in that success. Alderman Byrne was duly re-elected Lord Mayor, once again defeating Kathleen Clarke.

In 1936, Byrne's contemporary James Joyce wrote a letter to his grandson, Stephen, that has since been published as a short story called *The Cat and the Devil*. Joyce's tale is set in the small French town of Beaugency. When the devil builds a bridge to allow its residents to cross a river, he does so on condition that the first person who crosses the bridge will belong to him. After the devil builds the bridge, everyone from the town comes to inspect it, but no one dares to cross. The wily mayor of the town, Alfie Byrne, who 'always had a great golden chain round his neck even when he was fast asleep in bed with his knees in his mouth', throws water on a cat, thus encouraging it to cross the river, and into the arms of the devil. So the devil's plan is thwarted, and the people of the town can use the bridge for ever.

Joyce's vignette would do to amuse a child, but the story also invites us to reflect on Alfie Byrne's willingness to work with villains for the greater good. And while the mayor's unkind treatment of the cat is a mischaracterization – Byrne was an early champion of animal rights – Joyce captures the showboating style of a politician-businessman who pretended to have all the answers.[13]

For several months leading up to the coronation of King George VI in May 1937, there was intense speculation as to whether Byrne would go to London for the festivities. On 27 April, the Lord Mayor received a politely worded threat:

A Chara:

The attention of the National Association of the Old I.R.A. has been drawn to the report that the Lord Mayor of Dublin, Alderman Byrne, intends to go to London for the purpose of taking part in the ceremonies in connection with the Coronation of George the Sixth of England.

I am directed by my Executive to point out to you that having regard to the relations at present existing between this country and England any such action by the Lord Mayor would be detrimental to the interests of the Irish Nation.

In view of the unanimous resolution passed at its recent Convention this organisation will use every endeavour to have removed from public office any official who attends the ceremonies held in London in connection with the Coronation on the 12th of May.
Mise, le meas

George Lennon

The recipient was also under pressure in other quarters. According to the *Daily Express*, 'an irate Catholic alderman threatened to manhandle paunchy little hand-shaking "Alfie" Byrne, should he be so imperially-minded as to attempt to attend the Coronation'. The prime ministers of Australia, Canada, New Zealand and South Africa were there, but the Free State government decided to send no representative. Byrne responded with the same subterfuge that he had used for the funeral of King George V: 'Certain no Dublin alderman would object to his attending Mass, the guileful Lord Mayor hurried off to attend a special Coronation Pontifical High Mass at Westminster Cathedral.'[14] His strategy was described by the *Derry People*:

> Some of the old Unionist supporters of the Lord Mayor in the Corporation were pressing him to go to London for the Coronation. They were said to have hinted that if he did not go they would not vote for him [in the next Mayoral election]. An equal number of his Nationalist supporters laid down a contrary line of policy in equally emphatic terms.

This is just the kind of situation that his lordship loves. He succeeded in achieving the almost impossible feat of allaying the feeling of both sides by remaining away from London on the day of the Coronation and then going to London for the service in Westminster Cathedral.[15]

Byrne left Dublin on the mail-boat at eight, and was in London at six the following morning. Back in Dublin, 'crowds of Republicans demonstrated, police drew batons and charged, and in the resulting battle nearly every window in Henry Street was broken. For Coronation night was reserved the high-spot of Republican celebration, when a mine was used to blow up a statue of King George II in Dublin's Stephen's Green.'[16] For many months after the explosion, this ill-fated sculpture would lie on its side in the Lord Mayor's garden.

The Anglo-Irish relationship is the subject of some forensic waffle in a monologue filmed for Pathé Gazette in 1936. Sitting in the garden of the Mansion House, the Lord Mayor looks a bit stiff, even imperious. He is not above twisting his moustache. Addressing British viewers in a nasal whine, Byrne says he is wearing 'the same chain worn by Daniel O'Connell in 1847' (he meant 1841), then sermonizes on the subject of the border for six minutes without pause. Verbose and hectoring, Byrne does not endear himself to the camera. The only charming moment is when a cat runs across the garden. But the film is not a flattering artefact. It suggests that Byrne would have struggled in the age of the soundbite.

I cannot imagine prosperity coming to this country until by agreement that festering sore that is really a danger to our country as well as to England – I refer to the removal of the border between North and Southern Ireland – if we can get that border removed by consent and if our people as I said before will settle down, I am satisfied it will be to the benefit of England as well as to our people in Ireland . . . Now, if we hated each other a little less than what we do today, and if we did not exaggerate our admiration of those whom we agree with, and if we had a little less condemnation of our friends as well as our opponents I think it would be to the advantage of the whole country. This little country of ours cannot continue to keep two parliaments with two big sets of officials going, and if I can be of the slightest service now or at any time in bringing people together that will remove that border it will be the one ambition of my life and as I said already to you, I hope the day is not far distant when they will get together and think of the unemployed and think of the future of the country regardless of what it means to themselves and their public positions.

Jimmy O'Dea is the first signature in the Mansion House visitors' book for 1937.[17] Visitors that year included a group of businessmen from Manchester and a dog-trainer from Southampton. The essayist Hubert Butler brought a friend from Yugoslavia to meet the first citizen, while other guests included Theodore Roosevelt Jr and actor Dudley Digges. For all his windy speeches, Byrne was an accomplished host. Visitors were impressed by his charm and his courtesy, but also by the mayoralty and, by extension, Dublin. If civic pride is the amount of love that a place has for itself, the destiny of Dublin's loudest champion was to play the role of Cupid.

For the 1937 General Election, the size of some constituencies was reduced and, as a result, Byrne was deprived of nearly eight thousand votes in what the *Irish Times* called the 'gerrymandered constituency' of Dublin North-east.

Knowing that Fianna Fáil was scheming to unseat him, he decided to run the second eldest of his eight children as a candidate in the neighbouring area, Dublin North-west, to chase the 'missing' eight thousand votes. Alfred Byrne Junior – 'young Fred' to his family – was a twenty-four-year-old clerk at the time of his decision to run for public office. He would eventually qualify as a barrister.

According to the folklore of Dublin, it was a good-humoured election campaign. Many years later, an eighty-seven-year-old woman called Evelyn would ring *Liveline*, on RTÉ Radio, to share her memories of Jim Larkin giving a speech outside Gaffney's pub in Fairview. 'I know all the women in Marino will give Alfie Byrne their vote,' Larkin said, 'but I want the men.' At that point, Byrne himself spoke up from the crowd: 'Ah they'll vote for me alright, you needn't worry about that.' According to Evelyn, Byrne and Larkin 'had the bit of banter between them. It was friendly, they were having a laugh. There was no anger or anything in it.'

On the eve of the election, the *Daily Express* conducted an interview with the Lord Mayor, 'the sole surviving political link between Westminster and the Dáil'. Byrne was 'the thimbleful of sherry in the wine list of Irish politics', but readers were warned not to 'run away with the idea that Alderman Byrne is just a municipal comedian'.

> Now Mr Byrne is far more important than he might appear in the Irish political machine. Because, although he has always supported Mr Cosgrave in treaty matters, he has retained his independent status. This is a brave thing to do in the Free State today as many people have discovered to their cost. 'I am frankly for the British connection,' he told me in conversation tonight. 'I know England. I like England.'[18]

For the campaign, Byrne hired men to walk around the city as 'sandwich men for a double poster, one side of which advocates votes for the father, the other for the son'. This may be the origin of the tale that for one election the only campaigning he did was to send sandwich-men out with the slogan 'Alfie in danger', and it was enough to secure his seat.[19]

Byrne's Anglophilia was not the handicap his critics imagined. There was a residue of working-class Redmondite support near the docks but, more than that, *everyone* had family in England, and Byrne tried to improve the relationship at a time when his government was fighting a pointless Economic War. That enhanced his appeal not just in Dublin but throughout the country. On this occasion he was, in fact, the first candidate elected in the state, topping the poll in Dublin North-east. Larkin was returned on the final count. As a result, Fine Gael's Richard Mulcahy was not re-elected, and this damaged Byrne's relationship with the party: he was blamed for the defeat of Mulcahy and also of another candidate in Dublin North-west, where young Fred took a seat. After a long period of beneficial co-operation between Byrne and Fine Gael, these election results created bad feeling that would persist for over a decade.

The election of 'The Two Alfies' made headlines: it was the first time a father and a son sat together in Dáil Éireann. 'And all this was achieved in a very unostentatious way,' reported the *Wicklow People*. 'The Lord Mayor had no poll clerks in the polling station, he held no public meetings, made no speeches, and used no transports of any kind. Alfred Junior had one car to go around in, and the Lord Mayor had another. All the Lord Mayor's posting work was done with banners and sandwich boards.' Voter turnout was low among the working class, and trade union membership was dwindling. That is the context, writes Tom Garvin, in which Byrne 'virtually founded a political dynasty on an "anti-political" non-party platform'.[20]

The meeting to elect a new Lord Mayor was a rancorous affair, with 'stormy scenes and many interruptions from the gallery'. Éamonn Cooney of Fianna Fáil said he had opposed Byrne's re-election the previous year because he feared that Byrne intended to go to the Coronation. 'Alderman Byrne did the next best thing. He arrived in London the following morning and made a gallant effort to shake hands with the newly-crowned king. He represents the Empire mind in the city and it is an insult to have him fill the office of Lord Mayor.'[21]

Patrick Byrne believes that his father's greatest political achievement was to prevent Fianna Fáil from controlling Dublin Corporation in the 1930s. On this occasion, Tom Kelly accused him of 'endeavouring to control Dublin for the Byrne family'.[22] Byrne won anyway, once again defeating Kathleen Clarke.

In 1937, the first set of traffic lights in Dublin was installed at the junction of Clare Street and Merrion Square. That summer was so muggy that a visitor, V. S. Pritchett, complained of picking up fleas on a northside tram. In August, at the height of what is now called the silly season, Alfie Byrne found himself at the centre of a national controversy.

During the 1920s, there were more children in 'industrial schools' – reformatories – in the Irish Free State than there were in England, Scotland, Wales and Northern Ireland combined.[23] A man once told Byrne about his time in one of these institutions: 'I suffered untold agony there for two and a half years, I was beaten with the catoninetails for using tobacco, I had scars twelve inches long on my back for three months. I still carry a hunch on my back from that flogging.'[24]

By 1937, children as young as eight years old were being sentenced to spend up to five years in an industrial school for crimes as trivial as stealing a few apples from an orchard.[25] On 21 August, Byrne opened the North Dublin Horticultural Society Show in the grounds of St Patrick's Training College, Drumcondra. In his speech, the Lord Mayor appealed for common sense in the punishment of children caught 'boxing the fox', a common term for stealing apples:

> Whilst we all take pride in our gardens, and resent very much any interference with them, I think every human being in this city will agree that the sentences imposed upon children from eight to eleven years of age within the past few days were very savage indeed . . . We read that children of these tender years have been taken from their parents and put into schools out of the way for a period of from three to five years . . . I will venture to say that there is hardly a grown-up person in these grounds who, sometime or other in their childhood days, did not in an innocent manner interfere with a garden or an orchard . . . I hope that the children will be released and go back to the proper authority of their parents who can best look after them.

Byrne's description of the sentences as 'very savage' incensed the judiciary and the Catholic Church, which controlled many of the institutions where children were incarcerated. Senior Justice Little – the pre-eminent judge on the District Court – responded with a bullish defence of the industrial school system, and urged an end to 'this ridiculous Mansion House mummery'.[26] But Byrne stood firm: 'All I want to do is to express my opinion that for the punishment of trifling offences the home of the children is better than any institution. I do not like the children being taken from under their parents' roof.'[27]

Byrne found himself on the wrong side of the press. Most papers echoed the *Catholic Herald*, which provided a stout defence of the religious orders that controlled the industrial schools. Further, the prevalence of juvenile crime was 'appalling'. There was 'a veritable epidemic' of orchard-robbing. The author ends with a proposition that no sensible person could deny. 'Is anything but the reformatory suitable to such cases?'[28] The *Evening Mail* adopted an equally pugnacious tone:

> It is all very well to talk of the cruelty of depriving parents of their children; but it is clear that in many of these cases it is all to the children's good, and that in an institution they will have a much better chance of growing up into useful citizens than if left to run wild through the city and suburbs causing trouble and annoyance to everybody.[29]

The *Waterford Star* joined papers around the country in condemning 'the over-photographed and over-rated Lord Mayor of Dublin'. Magistrates were 'far too lenient with youthful offenders of both sexes'. As for the mayor: 'No, Mr Byrne, your oratory on this occasion does not cut any ice. It is nearly as tiresome as that chain of office which the daily newspapers force us to gaze on daily.' The *Irish Times*, too, saw fit to wag a finger: 'Many of the young blackguards who wreck gardens and despoil orchards deserve the most condign punishment. Their parents obviously are not able to keep them under proper control and some form of discipline is essential if they are not to grow up without any respect for their neighbour's rights.'

Encouraged by support in the press, Justice Little went on the attack again, lamenting Byrne's 'grotesque misrepresentation of the functions of the industrial school system'. It was, he said, 'an expression of the Christian office in praise of discipline'. And what about the teachers in such institutions? Did they deserve to be applauded? 'The management of those schools was the life work of men and women of gentle breeding who had given up all to devote themselves to the care and education of those children of the poor.'[30]

Now on the back foot, Byrne said a committee should be set up to deal with errant children outside the judicial system. Only the *Church of Ireland Gazette* dared to support the proposal: 'Most people will agree with him that it is a very severe sentence to send a child to an industrial school for a very small offence, unless adequate investigation has shown that the home is so unsuitable that the child has a better chance of a useful life if taken away from it.'

The incident led to reforms of the children's court, including the hearing of cases in camera. This step was taken for the sake of children and their parents, but also, the *Evening Herald* noted, 'to protect from humiliation the nuns and brothers and Religious Orders – the authorities responsible for the management of the approved schools'.[31] And the notorious Black Maria police van would no longer be used to transport children from the court. Byrne claimed victory: 'All the abuse and misrepresentation that I have received in the last week or two have been worthwhile because of this reform,' he said. 'And more reform must come.'[32]

Summer turned to autumn, more traffic lights were erected, and, whenever the subject was mentioned again, many Irish people were happy to defend the industrial schools. Approximately 170,000 Irish children were detained in them between

1936 and 1970.[33] Although it was not a popular issue, Byrne continued to campaign around the edges of this subject for many years. He was not the sort of person who thought that history would judge his generation for the mass incarceration of children. He just thought the system was too harsh.

In 1954, at the age of seventy-two, Byrne received a letter from a woman in Whitehall. 'Due to your kind representation to the Minister for Education, my son was released from Daingean Reformatory yesterday.'[34] Byrne deserves credit for continuing to fight such battles, although his optimism in 1937 was misplaced. Reform of the industrial schools came far too slowly for the victims of a vile system that locked kids up and abused them at will.

13. Alfie for President

In 1936, Éamon de Valera sat down to write a new Constitution. His goal was to replace the Constitution of 1922 with a document that embodied the Catholic nationalist tradition. It would take nearly a year to complete. Bunreacht na hÉireann was produced with the assistance of senior civil servants and the input of Church leaders of all faiths, but conspicuously reflected and reinforced the position of the Catholic Church at the heart of Irish life. De Valera described the new Constitution as 'the spiritual and cultural embodiment of the Irish people'.[1]

The Constitution was ratified by referendum on 1 July 1937, the same day as the general election. Article 57.1 stipulated that the first President of Ireland should enter office not later than 180 days after the Constitution came into force. The salary for the position was a generous £15,000. Who, then, should fill this exalted position?

Byrne was mentioned in connection with the presidency even before the Constitution had been ratified by the electorate. This speculation happened with his blessing and probably with his active involvement. Four weeks after the Constitution was approved, the *Sunday Chronicle* predicted that Byrne's 'enormous following may yet send him to be the first President of Éire'[2] and, as the year dragged on, speculation became more fevered. Here is the *Midland Tribune*:

Will 'Our Alfie' be the first President of Ireland under the new constitution? Because of his recent excursions to the country and his increased activity in the city, it is taken for granted that he has decided to be first in the field in the race for the exalted position. Within a few weeks he has taken pains to project himself into the public eye in counties as far apart as Tipperary, Carlow, Tyrone and Cavan. In Cavan, last week, he spent a considerable time one day inspecting creameries and shaking hands with local big-wigs. Hard-headed and cynical politicians here argue that a Lord Mayor of Dublin does not go into the country merely to see the green fields.[3]

By November, the papers were profiling the likely runners in a race that would not be held until the following spring. Seán T. O'Kelly – whose title would change from Vice-president of the Executive Council to Tánaiste under the new Constitution – was keen for the job, and he was de Valera's favoured candidate, but there was a problem: O'Kelly had been bested by Byrne on five of the six occasions they had run in the same constituency. Leslie Luke of the *Sunday Chronicle* confirmed that Byrne was the most 'dangerous' opponent any presidential candidate of Fianna Fáil could meet:

Mr de Valera, even without the backing of the great party machine he controls, could most probably beat [Byrne]. No other Fianna Fáil candidate . . . could even be reasonably sure of success against Alfie – unless the Fianna Fáil machine were working full-throttle behind him. If Fianna Fáil thus opposed Alfie it is quite probable that Mr Cosgrave's . . . party would forget past differences with the Lord Mayor and back him with full force. The Presidential election would thus become what Mr de Valera earnestly and anxiously seeks to avoid, a political Donnybrook on a country-wide scale, and his high hopes for inaugurating an ideal presidency with a new unpolitical contest would die . . .

Byrne was reportedly visited several times a day by people who wanted him to announce his candidature. 'They all ask directly "Will you go forward for the presidency, or not, Lord Mayor?" Alfie only smiles in answer.'[4] But Fine Gael – still sore about the general election – was having second thoughts about backing Byrne: 'According to the latest rumours, the leaders in 3 Merrion Square are considering abandoning their previous decision not to run any candidate.'[5]

While there was no constitutional ban on parties nominating their own candidates, a notion took hold that the President should be above politics. Initially, at least, Fianna Fáil rejected what it perceived as an unwelcome idea. Addressing his party's ard fheis in October 1937, Éamon de Valera defended its right to nominate a candidate:

> We shall do everything to give to the Irish state a head that will be worthy of the Irish state; and when he has been elected by the people in a free election we hope that all parties will give him the loyalty and reverence which are due to the man who will be chosen to represent Ireland . . .

Eventually, under pressure to declare his intentions, Byrne threw his hat into the ring. On 6 December 1937, the *Irish Times* noted that 'He declined to discuss his prospects or whether his nomination will come from the Cosgrave Party or be made on an Independent basis.' In retrospect, showing his hand before the question of party support was resolved seems a naïve course of action. Byrne may have thought that Fine Gael would soon throw its weight behind him, or that other contenders would be discouraged by his declaration. Or he may have been trying to force the matter with his old friend Cosgrave.

That Christmas was, as always, a giddy time in the social

life of Dublin, and the Lord Mayor was over-extended, with commitments to attend dozens of balls, dances and parties over the festive season. His presence lent glamour to proceedings. Meet the mayor in a rush to give Dublin his blessing:

> He was on his way to say a few words to yet another meeting, the fourth of fifth in his night, and he whispered to me . . . 'What's going on here? What meeting is this?' Even as he spoke he was bowing from left to right to acknowledge the applause. In a moment he was on the stage, saying the right thing about the right thing. [That] was one moment of his life when he was majestic.[6]

On the night of 17 December, when the government tried to adjourn a debate in the Dáil until the new year, Byrne shouted, 'The Minister has told us nothing about the 90,000 unemployed in the city of Dublin.' The intervention would have been more credible if he had not been on the way to a gala ball. Seán Lemass said, 'I am not going to give way to Deputy Byrne. He comes in here to talk about the unemployed wearing a dress suit.' Byrne interrupted, but Lemass was not in the mood. 'Now that Deputy Byrne has made his demonstration, let him go out to his dance.' This was not a good moment for Byrne, who was still shouting about the starving poor as the other deputies were leaving the chamber.[7]

The following day an editorial in the *Irish Times* lamented what was shaping up to be a public battle for a position that was supposed to be above party politics. The paper predicted 'a straight fight between two men' – Byrne and O'Kelly. After acknowledging that 'both of the gentlemen have admirable qualities', an appeal was made to common sense:

This country has a bad record in the matter of political elections. Personal abuse and mud-slinging are part and parcel of the system. We do not suggest that either of the prospective candidates would stoop to such methods, but what of their supporters? We would appeal to Messrs de Valera and Cosgrave to come together and nominate a joint candidate. Surely, this is an occasion for agreement.

On St Stephen's Day, Byrne made an appeal on the radio for the Sick and Indigent Roomkeepers' Society. Then he entertained three thousand inmates of the Dublin Union, hiring five bands to play at a total cost of five hundred pounds. On Henry Street the next day, he 'walked right up to Father Christmas amid a crowd of working-class shoppers, shook hands with him and ordered toys for every child about him'.[8] That week the *Daily Mail* called him a certainty for the presidency. The other candidates had none of his broad appeal, and in the new year he would go on a nationwide tour. There was talk of the Freedom of Kilkenny as well as other garlands. The presidency would be the culmination of a long and distinguished career of public service.

On 29 December 1937, the new Constitution came into effect. On New Year's Day, the Lord Mayor of Dublin did the honours at the Cab Derby in Phoenix Park. One of the most imposing sights in the park was the Viceregal Lodge, which would soon serve as the official residence of the new head of state. With any luck, the mansion (now re-named Áras an Uachtaráin) would be the Byrne family home by the following summer.

The following day, Cardinal Joseph MacRory, Archbishop of Armagh and Primate of All Ireland, said in a sermon that the President should really be agreed upon without an election. In other words, the Catholic Church did not want a full-scale competition. He might have been parroting the *Irish Times* when he said:

> The President will be expected to be outside, and above, all parties, but if he should be a nominee of a party, there will always be a danger of suspicion that he will favour that party. If, on the other hand, an agreed candidate could be found, it would be an object lesson in unity, and might have far-reaching results.

The Cardinal's intervention carried far more weight than an *Irish Times* editorial. It was not helpful to an independent politician who must have fancied his chances before the electorate. The sermon, which was dutifully parsed in every national daily, immediately complicated Byrne's position. The *Evening Mail* outlined the new reality:

> At the moment gossip has it there will be two candidates: Mr Seán T. O'Kelly as the Fianna Fáil nominee, and the Lord Mayor of Dublin as his opponent . . . Both are men of great ability, both are patriots whose sincerity none can doubt, and if their lives had been passed in paths other than those they selected, we can readily believe that either would have been a suitable choice for the presidency. But the fact is that both are politicians of opposing hue. An election would mean the putting into motion of the re-creation of all the bitterness associated with a general election: and the great and aloof position of President would be dragged in the political dust and suffer the very indignity that the author of the Constitution is most anxious it should not suffer. An appointment upon which all parties can agree is in our opinion a necessity of the position.

There is no record of Byrne's private response to the Cardinal's intervention, nor any evidence to suggest that the Cardinal was exacting revenge for the Lord Mayor's criticism of the industrial school system. Byrne must have known, in any case, that the sermon was unhelpful. In public, he renewed his efforts to win support, including from the Cardinal. On 19 January, when His Eminence arrived in Dublin, to attend a production of *As You Like It* at the Dominican Convent in Donnybrook, the Lord Mayor kissed his ring on bended knee. The *Evening Herald* noted, with one eye raised, 'The Cardinal's visit to Dublin is described as a surprise – interesting in the context of the Cardinal's intervention in the Presidential race.' The battle was just beginning. And nothing in Alfie Byrne's career – not even losing his seat at Westminster – quite prepared him for it. A 'Dublin Letter' in the *Frontier Sentinel* outlined the scale of the challenge:

> The one man who stands most to lose by an agreed election is the Lord Mayor of Dublin. His chances of being selected as an agreed candidate are negligible. The Lord Mayor is not popular with the politicians and never has been. He is too much of an individualist to be a good Party man, or to work well as a cog in the Party machine. His popularity with the people is unquestioned, and he is easily the most popular man in Dublin . . . The Lord Mayor is determined to contest the presidency, but he is far too shrewd a man to stand outside an agreement of the kind suggested by the Cardinal.[9]

Byrne could be peevish under assault. When an influential observer, Lord Ashbourne, spoke in favour of Byrne's rival for the post, Seán T. O'Kelly, 'because he speaks Gaelic', and because O'Kelly 'understands Irish problems better', Byrne

wrote an agitated letter to the editor of the *Irish Independent*.
The letter starts slowly ('During my thirty years in public
life . . .') and concludes with a sermon:

> Much has been written with reference to the possibility of a
> non-political agreed candidate being found for that high
> honour. Personally, I have tried to be as non-political as any
> man in this country. I have received representatives of every
> religious group, making no distinction between class or
> creed, and as long as I am in the Mansion House I will never
> make such distinction. I have received visitors from all over
> the world, with letters of introduction from various people.
> I never stood for religious or political intolerance, and never
> shall. I visited England on dozens of occasions within the
> past few years, doing my utmost to make friends for Irish
> people, and on more than one occasion I was warned against
> doing so, and my reply to those who warned me was that I
> was only a little in advance in visiting England, and that I
> thought I represented the vast majority of our people in so
> doing. I am of the opinion that a candidate for presidency
> should be prepared to work in complete harmony with the
> Government of the country, no matter from what political
> party the Government may come. I believe I could work in
> harmony with the present or any Government which might
> follow them. Having regard to all the facts as set out above,
> I cannot agree with Lord Ashbourne that Mr S. T. O'Kelly
> understands Irish problems better than I do.[10]

In the absence of a commitment from Fine Gael, Byrne
embarked on a tour of the country, trying to convince county
councils to back his nomination. In Kilkenny, he received
the Freedom of the City. In Cork, he made a tour of some
factories and new housing. (With typical overstatement, he

said it was 'the busiest and most interesting forty-eight hours I have ever spent'.)[11] The *Daily Sketch* reported:

> [The Lord Mayor] has broken his own record for hand-shaking, he has been to a race meeting for the first time in years, and he has gone down to Connemara to patronise a dance. And that's the way which leads to the Presidential Palace, say shrewd observers. Only a comprehensive peace treaty with Britain would secure the return of Mr De Valera's nominee, expected to be Mr Seán T. O'Kelly.[12]

But – perhaps inevitably – the Cardinal got his way. After nearly a year of talking about a presidential election, Fianna Fáil decided to change direction. A meeting of the party on 7 April concluded with a resolution to find a candidate acceptable to each of the major political parties. While sceptical that de Valera would consent to the appointment of anyone who was not a creature of his own, Fine Gael stressed that it also agreed with Cardinal MacRory. This admission was critical, because everyone in Leinster House knew that Fianna Fáil would never agree to support Alfie Byrne as a unity candidate. In deferring to the Cardinal's wishes, Fine Gael was effectively abandoning the Lord Mayor. Perhaps Byrne had exhausted his goodwill with the party; perhaps they had more to fear from a politicized presidency; maybe the Cardinal applied additional pressure. Whatever the reasons, the Lord Mayor's position suddenly became quite hopeless.

But he did not give up. In order to get on the ballot, Byrne needed the support of twenty members of the Dáil, or else four county councils. When it was decided that nominations for the race would close on 4 May, because of an order made by none other than the Minister for Local Government, Seán T. O'Kelly, Byrne complained that he did not have enough time to convince four county councils to support his nomination, as they would not hold their monthly meetings until the first week in May. Still he kept fighting. On 14 April, the *Sunday Independent* assured readers that he would not give up, 'whether the political parties agree on a candidate or not, excepting always that the candidate be Mr de Valera or Mr Cosgrave. In that instance the Lord Mayor would not stand.' Byrne also 'criticised the short time allowed for the campaign. A candidate would require an aeroplane to get around all the constituencies in the short time allowed.'[13]

On 21 April 1938, some of the most senior figures within Fine Gael and Fianna Fáil met in a day-long conference. Its purpose was to find a candidate who might be agreeable to both parties, thus avoiding an election. That afternoon, Byrne spoke to the *Irish Times*. 'If the Prime Minister or ex-President Cosgrave contest the election, I will not be a candidate, but I do not see why I should be asked to stand aside for anybody else.'[14] (Whether Byrne said he would stand aside for de Valera or Cosgrave, or, as he told another paper that afternoon, 'for no one', is now a moot point.) That evening, the two largest political parties announced their decision to nominate Dr Douglas Hyde for the role of President. The following morning, the *Irish Times* reported:

> Seen last night by an *Irish Times* reporter, the Lord Mayor stated that he was not surprised at the news that Dr Hyde had been agreed upon by the two parties. Dr Hyde, he said, was a charming, cultured Irish gentleman. Asked if the agreement on Dr Hyde's nomination would affect his intention to offer himself as a candidate, Alderman Byrne said that at the moment he was not prepared to make any statement about future plans.

That same morning, Byrne told another reporter, 'Anything can happen before 4 May, nomination day.'[15] After lunch, he went out to open a sale of work in the Convent of Marie Reparatrice on Merrion Square, in aid of the Building Fund Committee. At four o'clock, as he walked into City Hall, Byrne was collared by two pressmen. Was he still going to run? The answer was no. Byrne was out of the race.

That evening, two emissaries arrived at the home of Douglas Hyde in Roscommon, greeted him in Irish, and presented an official letter asking him to accept the presidency. At the age of seventy-eight, Hyde worried that he might be too old for the position – but he eventually accepted the invitation. There was no need for an election, because only one man enjoyed enough support to get on to the ballot paper. Byrne was not the only candidate who had good reason to regret this outcome. For months, Éamon de Valera had supported his loyal deputy, Seán T. O'Kelly. What prompted the Taoiseach's decision to dump O'Kelly and do a deal with his enemies in Fine Gael? The *Birmingham Post* provided an answer:

So far there has been no attempt at an explanation of the dropping of Mr O'Kelly, although it is said that Mr de Valera desired to avoid party contest. Had his desire to avoid party controversy and a personal context been made manifest at an earlier stage, there could not have been any question of nominating Mr O'Kelly, who has been a severe partisan for the greater part of his political life. Some other explanation must be sought for the change of mind and heart made by Mr de Valera, and that explanation is undoubtedly the fear that Mr O'Kelly would have been defeated by the Lord Mayor of Dublin, whose popularity in all parts of the country is very marked. That is the only tenable explanation.[16]

Douglas Hyde was a Protestant nationalist who had opposed the Easter Rising and abhorred the Civil War. However, he was palatable to Fianna Fáil in large part because of his devotion to the Irish language. Declan Kiberd has written that the native tongue was often used 'as a kind of green spray-paint, useful in concealing the embarrassing similarity of Irish parliaments as well as Irish post-boxes to their English models'.[17] And nobody spoke grander Irish than Douglas Hyde. Shortly before his inauguration, the President-Elect shared his vision of an Irish-Ireland:

> I hope we shall now develop along the lines of a Gaelic nation . . . Gaelic not only in language but in music, games, literature and dancing. It may not come in my lifetime. It may not come in yours either. There are not as many people as I would like speaking Irish today, but I have insisted on having an Irish-speaking staff at the President's house. We are making progress, however, the children learn Irish in the schools, but the problem is to persuade them to continue its use as their mother tongue after they leave school.[18]

Hyde had, in fact, opposed de Valera's decision to make the study of Irish compulsory in schools. Disagreeing with what might be called the spray-paint approach to promoting the language, he thought persuasion would be more effective than compulsion, and he later clashed with the government on this question. In 1954, long after Hyde's death, another former luminary in the Gaelic League concluded, 'Douglas Hyde foresaw what has since come to pass – that resentment at the compulsion of "coercion Irish" would destroy all the interest and affection for Gaelic that the League had built up.'[19]

Seven days before Hyde was inaugurated as President, he accepted an invitation to pose outside Leinster House. He sits on a chair in a long overcoat and a dark suit. Standing behind him, there is a smaller figure in morning suit, wing collar, gold chain, tie and handkerchief. Alfie Byrne wears a moustache that is clipped, immaculate, fussy, unlike the large, bushy appendage on the face of the President-Elect. The Lord Mayor looks comfortable at the side of Dr Hyde, and they remained on very good terms.[20] But this was grace under pressure, for a strange combination of forces had just colluded to deprive Byrne of a crowning honour. A lesser man would have refused the invitation. The photograph captures his respect for decorum and his essential decency.

Douglas Hyde's election as President enabled the government to appear magnanimous at a time when many Protestants felt unwelcome in the land of their birth. The US ambassador to Britain, Joseph Kennedy, said Hyde's election was 'an act that is eloquent of that brotherhood and tolerance which remain the hope of mankind in an angry world'. *The New York Times* depicted the appointment as an expression of tolerance and magnanimity. However, when Hyde died in 1949, de Valera, John A. Costello and the rest of the Catholic political establishment – including Byrne – refused to enter a Protestant church for his funeral, because it was a reserved sin for a Catholic to attend a Protestant ceremony. Far from representing 'the hope of mankind in an angry world', Hyde's appointment reflected narrow political concerns.

Patrick Byrne believes that the first unsuccessful bid to become President was the greatest disappointment of his father's career. For the second time in his life, he was defeated by forces beyond his control, and for many years afterwards he refused to discuss the ordeal.

14. No More Shall We Hear of the Mansion House Rat

In April 1938, while Byrne was seeking to secure a nomination for the presidency, the Economic War with the United Kingdom came to an end. Éamon de Valera called another general election for 17 June, seeking to reinforce his democratic mandate. It was an unusually quiet campaign for Alfie Byrne. For once, he did not hurl himself at Dublin. Trailing behind Oscar Traynor (who secured 10,308 first-preference votes) and Richard Mulcahy (9,072), the *Irish Times* said Byrne (7,386) 'barely contrived to hold his [Dáil] seat' in the election. An editorial in the paper concluded:

> His incumbency of the Mansion House, to all appearances, is secure as ever. Yet it behoves even so popular a person as the Lord Mayor to step cautiously. As we think, he made an error when he announced his candidature for the Presidency of Ireland. The poor people of Dublin, who swear by 'Alfie' Byrne as their Lord Mayor, may not have been pleased at the indication that he was ready to leave them for the larger and more glorious sphere of the Presidency. Are we far wrong in construing the decline of his poll at the general election as a sign that his true field of action is not so much national as municipal: not so much Ireland as Dublin?

When Dublin Corporation met to choose a Lord Mayor, the paper speculated that, in addition to the usual robust challenge from Fianna Fáil, some Fine Gael members would welcome Byrne's dethronement.[1] The *Strabane Chronicle* reported a rumour that Byrne was about to retire, or that Fianna Fáil and Fine Gael would agree on another candidate.[2] In the event, neither of those things happened, and the Lord Mayor faced three challengers. His supporters pointed to a long record of public service, while detractors lamented his long term in office and large salary. There were several references to what the *Irish Press* called his 'disappointment at the selection of Dr Hyde for the Presidency instead of himself'.[3] Fianna Fáil's Éamonn Cooney taunted the mayor: 'The best thing the Fine Gael party ever did was to join hands with our party in electing Dr Hyde as President.' Byrne had, said Cooney, been let down by Fine Gael, and was 'sore at that and bitterly disappointed'.[4]

The Lord Mayor did not reply.

Proposing Kathleen Clarke, Alderman Tom Kelly said she would bring 'a spirit and an atmosphere of culture' to the Mansion House. 'Why,' he asked, 'did Alderman Byrne above all others deserve to be placed on the city throne year after year? Not for all the money in the Sweepstakes would I sit in the Mayoral Chair for eight years and keep a woman like Mrs Clarke out.'[5] The reference to the Sweepstakes may have been an attempt to embarrass Byrne, drawing attention to one of his more lucrative wheezes, but it had no effect on the outcome.

After two and a half hours' discussion, in which proposals were followed by counter-proposals, accusations and repudiations bandied about, political history dug up and re-interred, and personalities freely indulged in, Alderman A. Byrne, T.D., was re-elected Lord Mayor of Dublin for the ninth year in succession, at the quarterly meeting of Dublin Corporation last night.[6]

Cue time-honoured homilies in the press: 'There are those who sneer at him as a "showman",' wrote the *Evening Mail*, 'as if he were merely that; but these people fail to appreciate that it is a Lord Mayor's duty to be a showman, and Ald. Byrne is much more besides. He is the right man for the job, and Dublin knows it.' The *Irish Times* was equally complimentary. 'We are, frankly, glad that he has been returned once again to office, rather than the avowed representative of a political party.' On the day after his election, the Lord Mayor paid a courtesy call on the President.

In September 1938, Byrne visited Wales, where he told audiences there would be no peace in Ireland until the country was united once again. 'And it will only be united by peaceful methods.'[7] Days later, Adolf Hitler – having already incorporated Austria into the Third Reich – achieved the annexation of the Sudetenland, with the blessing of the United Kingdom and France. Neville Chamberlain hailed 'peace in our time', but war was seen to be coming, and on his return to Ireland Byrne was forced to assure Dubliners that the Corporation 'would do everything in its power to advance any plans for providing adequate air raid precautions'.[8]

That Christmas, the *Sunday Dispatch* ran a front-page story, headed 'New Pictures of Two Irish Leaders', with the President and the Lord Mayor of Dublin in separate 'at home' photo shoots. The position of Hyde on the top half of the page would have seemed only appropriate. The battle was over. Byrne cut the page out with a coarse pair of scissors, and this bittersweet souvenir remained in his desk for the rest of his life.

In January 1939, twelve months after the *Daily Mail* had called Alfie Byrne a certainty for the Presidency, the same paper revealed that he was 'not feeling too well recently, owing to the strain of his attending so many engagements, particularly during the Christmas season. It was considered that he needed a change and a rest. And with this object, he has crossed to England.' Now aged fifty-six, the zealous Alderman had devoted every waking hour to work, but the intense disappointment of the presidential race had taken a toll.

On his return to Dublin, the Lord Mayor hosted at his own expense an entertainment for 3,500 patients in the Dublin Union. The following morning, the *Irish Times* – in an article headlined 'Alderman Byrne's Hint' – reported that the Lord Mayor's retirement was 'foreshadowed' during his speech at the event: 'The strain of the last year had been so heavy, the correspondence so enormous, the number of callers who he had to meet so great . . . that it had all affected his health.' Byrne continued, 'I feel the time has come to say so to my many friends. However, next year, when we have a new Lord Mayor, I hope that the patients here will have the pleasure of meeting him under circumstances similar to those to-night.'[9] The headline in the *Irish Independent* was more direct: 'Lord Mayor Retiring'.[10]

That February, Byrne flew to Rome to attend the funeral of Pope Pius XI, whom he had met in 1933. He prolonged his stay in order to dine with Cardinal MacRory at the Irish College. There is no evidence that they discussed the presidential election, in which MacRory's intervention had arguably scuppered Byrne's chances.

That spring, Byrne wrote an article about Dublin for the London *Times*. The tone was pompous ('Our public lighting arrangements are as good as any to be found in most modern cities') but also valedictory. When a reporter from the *Evening Mail* met the Lord Mayor on a tram, they were both on their way to the Spring Show in the Royal Dublin Society. 'He told me that he will miss his strenuous round of duties, when his term of office as Lord Mayor is over; for he is not going forward again as a candidate at the next election which is this summer.'[11]

On 25 May, Byrne told an English newspaper, 'Nine years is enough for any man.'[12] The *Irish Times* wanted him to stay on: 'Our own hope is that the present Lord Mayor will be induced, at this eleventh hour, to reconsider his decision to retire.'[13] By that stage, two Fine Gael councillors had declared their intention to run for the office: Peadar Doyle and Patrick Belton. The *Longford Leader* fancied Belton (he was from Longford) but as the election approached, he struggled to secure support within his own party: 'There were mysterious conferences, much rushings here and there at late hours by members of all parties, and dark whisperings about the things this or that Corporator was trying to do.'[14] Meanwhile, Peadar Doyle could not muster enough support among independents, who effectively held the balance of power.

On the night of 23 June 1939, Fine Gael nominated Doyle as their first choice for Lord Mayor, and Fianna Fáil, as ever, nominated Kathleen Clarke. When Clarke won the first round of voting, Fine Gael put Patrick Belton forward. But Belton was 'betrayed' by two colleagues: one voted for the Fianna Fáil candidate, and the other walked out of the chamber just before the vote.[15] Seeing that, 'apparently, no decision was about to be arrived at', Byrne allowed his name to go forward.[16] That explanation was somewhat disingenuous, as Mrs Clarke had looked likely to win before Byrne's change of heart. It was received with derision in certain quarters: 'Next move was the proposal of Alfie once again, causing those who said he never really wanted to retire to nod their heads and say "What did we tell you?" '[17]

Before a decisive vote could be taken, the session was adjourned; the council would reconvene the following night. In theory, Byrne would go up for election in a straight race against Mrs Clarke. But he agreed to contest the vote only if a deputy mayor would be willing to spend one or two hours a day helping him to cope with the work.[18] Tom Kelly was indignant at the thought of a tenth term for Byrne, and said of his Fianna Fáil colleague Kathleen Clarke:

> Here is a woman who has fought this contest five or six times. Tonight she succeeds after two divisions and when the Lord Mayoralty is within her grasp it is taken from her by rotten diplomacy. For the last six weeks I have heard it whispered that in spite of all he said, Alderman Byrne would be re-elected for a tenth year of office. It is a perfect scandal, and there is certainly no decency or chivalry left.[19]

When the council reconvened, Byrne declined to go up against Kathleen Clarke. His decision to allow himself to be nominated had been a mistake. 'The past two years have been particularly arduous for me as Lord Mayor, and I would prefer to leave the position now. I want to thank all who stood by me and voted for me, and who were apparently ready to do so again.'[20]

Byrne was out of the race, and Alderman Doyle was back in. If, with Belton out of the running, Doyle could command the full support of Fine Gael, he would have a chance of winning. When the council was polled informally, Mrs Clarke got eighteen votes to Doyle's fifteen. Then came a formal division on a motion to elect Clarke as Lord Mayor. This finished seventeen for and seventeen against. As Lord

Mayor, Byrne had the casting vote.[21] As the *Northern Whig* recorded, 'The council waited tensely for Lord Mayor Byrne to record his vote against Mrs Clarke. Instead he gave it for her.'[22]

Byrne's decision to anoint his rival was met with a standing ovation throughout the Chamber. The victory shocked Mrs Clarke, who broke down in tears. Upon recovering her composure, she told Byrne that she would not wear the mayoral chain that had been presented to the city by King William of Orange. 'I will take the smaller chain instead.'[23] There were cheers from the gallery and cries of 'Long may you wear it!' as Alderman Byrne invested his successor with the smaller chain of office. Mrs Clarke said, 'I thank you all from the very bottom of my heart. I thank in a very special manner the man who, through his casting vote, has put me here.' Byrne had treated her graciously for many years. 'He never seemed to forget that I represent a man whom all Ireland honours,' she said, referring to Thomas Clarke. 'It is because I represent that man that I have been put in this chair.'[24]

Byrne thanked 'the people of Ireland, and the citizens of Dublin, for their unflinching loyalty, support and encouragement'. His farewell included this charming mea culpa: 'I am, of course, not unaware of the fact that, from time to time, I made the inevitable blunder, but the indulgence of a generously-minded public promptly enabled me to become oblivious of my shortcomings.'[25]

It took a week for Byrne to move all the gifts he had received over the previous nine years out of the Mansion House. These oblations included five gold keys, three silver trowels, a Sweepstakes drum in silver plate, and a nurse's outfit, complete with pen, pencil and thermometer.[26] Cissie

Byrne welcomed the departure. While she had become close friends with Mary O'Sullivan, the senior Corporation official who managed the building, Mrs Byrne had never enjoyed living in the Mansion House. She was, her son Patrick recalls, happy to leave.

The new mayor's first visitor was Éamon de Valera. He was glad to be rid of the Mansion House Rat, and to regain control of the Round Room, which had once hosted a fledgling Irish parliament. Mrs Clarke threw out the picture of Queen Victoria, along with three portraits of kings: 'I felt I could not sleep in the house until she was out of it, she had been so bitterly hostile to Ireland and everything Irish.' Early one morning, tram-passengers were surprised to see a row of oil paintings lined up along the railings on Dawson Street.[27] Byrne lamented this act of civic vandalism: 'There were treasures of art in [that] room that were held in admiration by an element of the people. We would like to see the whole of our people united and happy and contented with any changes that were not desirable.'[28]

Mrs Clarke would not be emulating her predecessor's social life. 'Alderman Byrne was a man of tremendous energy, and I could not possibly attend the number of functions that he managed to fit into one day.'[29] And she had no need for three secretaries. (A journalist spotted one 'wiping away a tear as she took a message' for Byrne.)[30] Clarke was unwell for most of her first term, although she did find time to make an appeal to Dubliners: use more Irish in daily life. The mayor, who did not speak the language herself, was friendly with the German Minister to Ireland, Eduard Hempel, for whom she hosted a dinner, and the Japanese ambassador, Setsuya Beppu, who gave her 'a flower on each 3 May, the anniversary of her husband's execution'.[31]

The end of Byrne's reign was widely lamented. When a reporter from the *Irish Times* spotted him on Grafton Street, he was 'horrified' to see him 'naked without his chain'. People gawked at the mayor-no-longer. 'He was talking to a friend and nodded unceasingly to the passers-by as of yore, but, for the first time in my life, I saw the second button of his waistcoat. If Dev strolled into the Dáil in a pair of shorts and a tennis racquet in his hand it would be no greater sacrilege. Others must have thought as I did; for all stared at the familiar figure.'[32]

Dublin Opinion marked the moment with a front-cover illustration of Alfie Byrne (with mayoral chain) shaking the hand of Alfie Byrne (without chain), under the headline, 'Alfie Atque Vale'. Newspapers printed readers' verse on the subject. In one effort, a Dubliner reflected on the relationship between Byrne and his enemies. Despite the showmanship and the self-serving machinations, his foes now realized that Byrne had an innate sense of decency. In the very last act of his record-breaking tenure, the miniature mayor had made himself a giant.

> Where are the vices that blackened thy cheek?
> O! Alfred the Great!
> 'Imperialist,' 'blueshirt,' 'Freemason' and 'sneak,'
> How changed is thy state!
> The arrows which flew round your mayoral head,
> The curse which hung o'er thy silver-lined bed
> Are changed into flowers and blessings instead:
> O! Alfred the Great!
>
> No more shall we hear of 'the Mansion House Rat',
> O! Alfred the Great!
> 'The traitor', 'the Faker', – goodbye to all that.
> No longer we hate.

Your virtues till now were all cloaked in the dark,
Your door for the poor was always a mark,
You've opened it now to the sweet widow Clarke –
So, Alfred! You're Great![33]

15. The Emergency

'Dogs are wise. They crawl away into a quiet corner
and lick their wounds and do not rejoin the world
until they are whole once more.'

Agatha Christie

In the summer of 1939, after leaving the Mansion House and
before the outbreak of the Second World War, Alfie Byrne
took off for England on a goodwill tour. In diplomatic terms,
it was Mission Improbable: to convince the British to return
the six counties to Ireland. 'I am sure,' he said, 'that when the
facts are logically argued and understood it will be seen that
the abolition of the Border would be in the best interests not
just of the two countries directly concerned but also of the
entire Commonwealth.'[1] As usual, he was received with
respect and patience by English audiences. As ever, his argu-
ment for a united Ireland had precisely no effect.

Upon his return to Dublin, Byrne was invited to officiate
at dinners, dances and bazaars in his new role as Lord Mayor
emeritus. Missing the splendour of the mayoral chain, he
bought a large pocket watch on a gold chain. There were
speeches to be given in Cork, Belfast and Donnycarney, and
for a time, at least, he would remain one of Dublin's Most
Invited.[2]

The most celebrated biographer of Alfie Byrne's Dublin
had the power to make people live for ever. If you went to

school with him, all the better. There are several references to Alfie Byrne in James Joyce's last novel, *Finnegans Wake*, which was published in 1939. His name is transmuted into the opening letters of the Greek alphabet, 'alfi byrni gamman dealter etcera zezera'; he is also the 'Meynhir Mayour, our boorgomaister . . . his head hoisted, in best bib and tucker'. There is also a heading, 'Why we all Love our Little Lord Mayor.'[3] Like many Dubliners who wrote nothing about themselves, the mayor was immortalized in print by Joyce, whose posthumous manifestations in Dublin include the pub that Byrne once owned on Talbot Street. The site of the Verdon Bar is today occupied by the Ripley Court Hotel, which has a bar called the Ulysses Lounge.

After living in the Mansion House for such a long time, it was hard to find a property that quite compared for grandeur or convenience. Eventually, Byrne bought Williamsfort, a large Victorian home on Temple Gardens in Rathmines. However, Cissie thought it was too draughty, so the family moved into a very large house on Palmerston Road, a short distance away. In middle age, Byrne chose to live in one of the most salubrious parts of the city, and he often socialized with the winners in Irish society – the politicians, doctors, businessmen, bankers and lawyers who became the new establishment.

The purchase of the house on Palmerston Road left Byrne a bit short of cash. In February 1940, his bank manager warned him that his overdraft stood at £5,176. The bank manager also noted, perhaps pointedly, that 'the value of your stock exchange securities is £6,048'. A few months later, the manager wrote again: 'I think it well to bring to your notice that the price of Courtaulds is slipping back. They were 38/- when you went to England and are down to 32/7½ today.' Byrne sold his shares in Courtaulds and British American Tobacco in order to bring down the overdraft.[4] It was a temporary measure. If all went well, he would sell the house in 1945, the year of the next presidential election. Rathmines was a fine suburb for a member of the establishment, but it would be preferable to inhabit a large Georgian mansion in the middle of Phoenix Park. He wanted to return to the northside on his own rather grandiose terms.

For a brief period following his departure from the Mansion House, Byrne made a sincere effort to slow down for the good of his health. Restricting himself to one dance on a Friday, he subscribed to *Time* magazine, and even started to read novels. Agatha Christie was his favourite author. (He once told his son Patrick that he had met Hercule Poirot. 'It didn't seem fair to point out that Poirot was a fictional character,' Patrick recalls.) It could never last, and it didn't. After a few weeks of mild recuperation, Byrne returned to the Dáil with new vigour. Could the Electricity Supply Board supply the capital with free public lighting for twenty years? No? What about air-raid shelters near seaside areas? Free milk for schools? Don't get Alfie Byrne started on 'the noise caused by the Pigeon House generating plant'.[5]

Once again, Byrne succumbed to exhaustion: in November 1939 and again in April 1940, he was taken ill. The second episode started in the middle of a fractious debate in the Corporation. And in February 1940 he was the subject of an attack in the Dáil, when the Minister for Industry and Commerce, Seán MacEntee, castigated his record as Lord Mayor. James Dillon and Michael Brennan of Fine Gael jumped to his defence, along with an independent, Joe Hannigan, but MacEntee was determined to have his say.

MACENTEE: Deputy Alfred Byrne talked about people going into mental homes in consequence of the position existing in Dublin, and wanted to know where it was all going to end. For ten years the deputy held a position in Dublin the nearest analogy to which is that of an American city boss, and during that period he drew remarkable emoluments from the city.

DILLON: And spent far more on the poor of the city.

MACENTEE: He had time to meet and greet and to be photographed with every freak, fake and fraud that came here.

DILLON: He did far more for the city of Dublin in a week than the Minister did in his whole lifetime.

BRENNAN: Is there anything that the Minister will not stoop to?

MACENTEE: I would like Deputy Byrne to read the report of the Local Government Auditor upon the administration of the City of Dublin during the period when he was Lord Mayor, when he was supposed to look after the city and was the only check and guardian which the ratepayers of Dublin might have in regard to the way the Corporation was run, and ask himself if he is justified in coming here and making the sickening hypocritical speeches which he makes from time to time.

DILLON: Ask the poor of Dublin what they think, and they will give you their answer.

HANNIGAN: The Minister is surely aware that there was a city manager for the full period of Alderman Byrne's mayoralty.

MACENTEE: Alderman Byrne should examine his conscience and see how the city progressed when he was its chief magistrate.[6]

As the Wehrmacht swept across Europe, Ireland remained neutral during the Second World War, or the Emergency, as it was known. Most politicians, including Byrne, supported this decision. Terence Brown has written, 'There was a general concern that come what may, the victories won in 1921 should not be thrown away in wartime alliances and risky partnerships.'[7] Survival was the ultimate objective; in this regard the policy was successful, as the country was never invaded. And compared with the residents of many European capitals, Dubliners endured only minor hardship. There was no occupation, nor the terror of nightly bombings. The relative freedom of life in the city, coupled with the presence of foreign agents and refugees from war-torn Europe, led one wag to call Dublin the Casablanca of the north. At a play in the Gate Theatre, Denis Ireland observed:

> In spite of flying bombs over London and war clouds over Europe, conversation sparkles, rumour seethes like a bath of acid . . . it is Bloomsbury translated so far West that no one would bat an eyelid if some of the authors, or the sprigs of nobility gone native in corduroy trousers, were suddenly to produce six-shooters and start shooting up the chandeliers.

The cost of living went up in Dublin, and unemployment made life more difficult still for many young people. At one point, Byrne proposed that jobless men should be paid to build a Blue Lagoon on a disused tram line, 'keeping in mind the possibilities of the Blue Lagoon as a post-war development'.[8] Emigration was the first choice for many school-leavers: over two hundred thousand went to England to join the Armed Forces or to help with the war effort in the factories.[9] Those left behind included 'aggressive little ladies of the Anglo-Irish persuasion', in the words of John Ryan, 'who were doing their bit for the Allied war effort by letting out the air in the tyres of the Japanese ambassador. As a further earnest of their belligerence, these diminutive amazons would save their tea and sugar rations from the F. M. Café or Mitchell's Tea Shop to send to "the boys in blue".'[10]

A Dubliner called Maureen Diskin, who worked in a bank on Grafton Street, later told a historian that bananas were not available to buy in shops during the Emergency. 'And I remember there was a thing called "banana essence". If you mashed up parsnips and fed some banana essence into the mixture you could nearly make yourself a banana sandwich.'[11] The import of luxuries such as soap and tobacco was also restricted, and there were grain shortages until the Allies did a deal in exchange for more Guinness. The American ambassador, David Gray, was not impressed by the trade-off. The black stuff was, he said, 'at the best a luxury and at worst a poison'.[12]

When rationing was introduced, TDs were entitled to buy more petrol than members of the public.[13] Byrne put the quota to good use by dispensing with his car and buying a motorized bicycle. Even at that time the contraption was an unusual sight on the streets of Dublin. The shortage of petrol was a benison for jarveys, whose horse-drawn carts came back into fashion. Veteran jarveys railed against newcomers to the trade. One old-timer cursed 'the bowsies, the blaggards, the men only coming into the job [who] give decent jarveys a bad name'.[14] Many of these arrivistes were dockers for whom there was now little work in the once-bustling port.

Most of Kathleen Clarke's first year as Lord Mayor was spent in a nursing home; at one point, Tom Kelly reported, it had been 'touch and go' with her. But she was welcomed back to the City Council after she recovered her health, and stood for re-election in the summer of 1940. 'She has had no opportunity of showing her paces,' Kelly said, arguing that she deserved a second term.[15] A majority of the members agreed, and Mrs Clarke was re-elected.

Writing in the *Irish Press*, Patrick Kavanagh described a city in which young boys sat fishing at midnight on a Ringsend quay wall, thousands of starlings convened on the trees of O'Connell Street, and pigs were driven down Abbey Street.[16] That was the context in which Alfie Byrne found time to table a motion to protect the Georgian architecture of Merrion Square. Concerned about 'the unsuitable and gaudy alterations' to the front of a house on the north side of the square, he wanted the council 'to have the blot removed . . . and prevent further damage'.[17] The *Evening Mail* addressed the matter, citing the poet John Betjeman, who spent some of the war in Dublin as the British press attaché:

> The front doors of our Georgian houses are, says Mr John Betjeman, 'among the wonders of the world for the diversity of their delicate designs and for their fanlights'. Hundreds, perhaps thousands, of these houses have been allowed to fall into decay and ruin . . . But there still remain many brilliant examples of private houses . . . and unfortunately, there would seem to be some persons in the community who would 'modernise' these dignified and historic structures . . . Alderman Byrne wants to have the original frontage restored as far as possible, and steps taken to prevent any further alterations of the kind being made.[18]

In January 1941, German planes dropped bombs on Terenure and the South Circular Road. And on the night of 31 May, thirty people were killed when the Luftwaffe pounded the North Strand. (One theory is that the Luftwaffe believed they were over Liverpool; the West German government later paid compensation.) Byrne was among the first visitors to the devastated area in the heart of his constituency. A report in the *Evening Mail* noted, 'With tears in his eyes Alderman A. Byrne, T.D., also comforted persons who had lost not only their whole material possessions but also many of their dear ones.'[19] He raised money for victims of the bombing, and later clashed with Seán T. O'Kelly on the subject. James Dillon – the only TD who openly called for Ireland to support the Allies – also featured in these Dáil exchanges:

DILLON: Isn't it true that the people are getting help from the Red Cross and the Corporation?

O'KELLY: Yes, and Deputy Byrne knows that.

DILLON: It might be well for the guidance of the people to mention that.

O'KELLY: Those organisations have been working for and looking after the people in that area as we have all seen. Deputy Byrne also knows it, but it is not for that reason that he raises this matter now.

BYRNE: I want to know where these people will get £20 to buy furniture . . .

CEANN COMHAIRLE: The Deputy will resume his seat . . . It is not on the Order Paper.

BYRNE: It ought to be. They are not getting any money.[20]

In the municipal elections of 1942, the *Irish Independent* noted 'the extraordinary personal poll of Ald. A. Byrne T.D. who secured three and a half quotas in Area Two'. Jim Larkin was also re-elected, with the Labour Party – to which

Larkin was now reconciled – becoming the biggest party on the City Council for the first time. A journalist sent this report from the count:

> Two of the biggest heaps growing by the minute, showed the friendly rivalry between candidates Byrne and Jim Larkin. Byrne watched it fascinated, leaning over the wooden railing separating candidates and public from the counting officers. I teased him that the hand that shook 'em was now at rest. 'Ah,' [he] said, 'all I could do this time was to cycle round and raise my hat with the one free hand!' And the jet black eyes laughed boyishly.[21]

With a general election looming, the *Longford Leader* reported, Fine Gael arrived at an understanding:

> General [Richard] Mulcahy was approved as the Fine Gael candidate against Mr Oscar Traynor in North West Dublin, and it was decided to support the candidature of Alderman Alfie Byrne also. In practice, this will work the other way around, because Alfie is sure of election again and his second preferences will be important to anyone who can get them.[22]

On St Patrick's Day 1943, Éamon de Valera made a treacly broadcast about 'that Ireland which we dreamed of'. It was full of quiet prejudice and lofty images of a place that existed only in one man's imagination. Dublin wasn't even mentioned. Rather, Dev's ideal Ireland was a defiantly rural place: ' . . . a land whose countryside would be bright with cosy homesteads, whose fields and villages would be joyous with the sounds of industry, with the romping of sturdy children, the contests of athletic youths and the laughter of happy maidens, whose firesides would be forums for the wisdom of serene old age'.

In the general election that June, the quota in Dublin North-east was 9,754. Byrne got 11,293 first-preference votes, coming second to Oscar Traynor in the three-seater. But the tactic of supporting Byrne didn't work out for Fine Gael: Richard Mulcahy was defeated. The two main parties both lost seats, as Labour, Clann na Talmhan and independents all made gains. Fianna Fáil lost its majority but retained a healthy plurality, and de Valera managed to form a minority government with much the same team. Less than three months later, General Mulcahy was among the attendees at the funeral of Byrne's mother, Fanny. Kathleen Clarke was also there to offer support to her erstwhile rival.

Later that year, it emerged that James Derwin, a civil servant, and John A. Corr, a former Fine Gael councillor, had offered electors cash bribes to vote for Charles Houlihan and Peter Trainor Kelly – the Royal Liver Friendly Society's Irish head – in the Seanad election. When Corr tried to bribe an undercover detective, posing as an elector, he was arrested, and a tribunal was set up, at which Derwin and Corr said they were procuring votes on behalf of Kelly, Houlihan and 'other unnamed persons'. When Byrne's name was mentioned, Corr objected, and insisted that Byrne was not guilty of procuring votes for anyone.[23] Byrne himself testified, 'There was no truth . . . that Corr, through [me], procured votes in the Senate election in 1943 for Senator P. T. Kelly . . . by means of bribery. It would be foolish after thirty-five years to take such a risk, and I would not do such a dishonourable thing.'[24] While the incident did not do any lasting damage to Byrne's reputation, it revealed flaws within the political system, and as a result, reforms were introduced, making the Seanad election process more transparent.

When Éamon de Valera called a snap election in 1944, in

an effort to regain a majority for Fianna Fáil, the *Evening Herald* predicted a dogfight between Byrne, Jim Larkin and Harry Colley for the second and third seats in Dublin North-east.[25] In the event, Byrne took the second seat comfortably, and Traynor's surplus ensured Colley's seat.[26] Jim Larkin lost his seat – as did Alfie Junior in Dublin North-west, where he had been a TD since 1937.

That September, in the council chamber, Alderman Byrne had a problem on his mind: vermin. The trouble started on a bus, when a passenger opened a leather bag to reveal five dead rats. The city was, she said, infested. Then Byrne was called over to look at a baby's rat-bitten nose. Anxious families had to stay up all night, he told the council. Rats were taking over. It was an emotive account, but Larkin was not impressed:

> If you're out at three in the morning you'll meet regiments of [rats] marching along the roads. Everyone in the city is threatened, because it is an old city. When buildings are demolished they move on to inhabited places. Food areas are infested. You could sit down and take your tea with them. But, as everyone knows this, and as it has been before the Corporation times out of number, isn't Alderman Byrne only looking for publicity by bringing them out again?[27]

Larkin was correct. Byrne was grandstanding. That behaviour was typical because it had to be: in Ireland, local government was weak. While it is true that Byrne devoted his life to public service, it is also true that he never had that much clout. He was able to champion endless public spending because he never had to find the money to pay for it.[28] As we have seen, when his rivals on the left attacked him, it was not because they disagreed with him on these matters, but because he stole their clothes. 'I was the first to demand free schools, free school books, free footwear,' he often told constituents. 'I continue to advocate the hot school meal, and brighter and more playing fields and playgrounds and Housing Schemes in the city.' (This author once described Byrne as Tony Gregory in a top hat. A left-wing TD said the comparison was unfair to that noted champion of the working classes. But Gregory was, in fact, an admirer of Byrne.)[29]

Towards the end of the war, Douglas Hyde, who was practically bedridden, decided not to seek re-election as President. In the summer of 1945, de Valera nominated his loyal deputy, Seán T. O'Kelly, whose presidential chances he had scuppered first time around. Fine Gael nominated Seán MacEoin, a hero of the War of Independence; and a third veteran of that conflict, Patrick McCartan, stood as an independent. Byrne fancied a run himself. After failing to get on to the ticket through the Dáil, he tried to secure the support of four county councils. That did not go very well:

> Because of the strong political control that has entered into local Councils it appears impossible for one outside the political parties to get a nomination, and strong efforts are being made to prevent me getting an opportunity to go to the starting post. I am, however, hopeful, and believe that there are many members of the local Councils who are satisfied that the election of President should not be a party issue. It is to them I look for tolerance and goodwill and hope for the nominations before May 16 that will enable me to face the electors of Éire.[30]

The appeal was unsuccessful. At some county council meetings, his telegrams seeking support were not even read out. In Leitrim, his seconder arrived too late, while at

Westmeath the councillors voted to nominate no one.[31] When the nominations closed on 16 May, Byrne did not have enough support. O'Kelly went on to win a bitterly fought election. Having once replaced Hyde as the head of the Gaelic League, now he replaced him as President of Ireland.

During the war, life in Dublin was not as placid as it appeared to the outside world; but neutrality and censorship put the city in a strange limbo. 'It was as if an entire people had been condemned to live in Plato's cave,' wrote F. S. L. Lyons, 'with their backs to the fire of life and deriving their only knowledge of what went on outside from the flickering shadows thrown on the wall before their eyes by the men and women who passed to and fro behind them.' At the end of the war the cave-dwellers of Dublin emerged, blinking, into 'a new and vastly different world.'[32]

Byrne was sixty-three years old. Still devoted to public service, from time to time he would wonder if the mayoral crown had been passed too quickly.[33] Nine years in the Mansion House was a record that would never be broken, and he was proud of this achievement, but there was also regret about the manner of his departure. It is not fanciful to imagine that he felt like a great actor who had been hustled off the stage before the final act. And now that the Park was out of his sights, Dawson Street came back into view.

16. Coldest Winter Ever

'Will you please send me on five pounds as I
want to get in some turf as the weather is very cold,
we are after having an awful few weeks with
snow and frost and what I had in is almost gone
so please send it as soon as possible.'
Letter to Byrne from a woman in Ballinrobe,
Co. Mayo, March 1947[1]

Anthony Cronin wrote of post-war Dublin, 'The malaise that seems to have affected everywhere in the aftermath of war took strange forms there, perhaps for the reason that the war itself had been a sort of ghastly unreality. Neutrality had left a wound, set up complexes in many, including myself, which the war did little to cure.' Lip service was paid to Irish unity and the Irish language. 'Pieties, religious and patriotic, were the staple of every occasion. If it sounds boring, it was.'[2]

In 1946, Alfie Byrne told the Dáil that housing conditions in Dublin were the worst in Europe: 'At least 20,000 flats and 10,000 cottages are needed in the city to meet requirements.'[3] He had form letters printed by the thousand: 'Dear Sir, It is with regret that I have to inform you that my efforts to secure employment for you have failed.' Byrne and his old rival, Jim Larkin, still sold themselves as champions of the poor, despite the fact that they lived on two of the finest residential streets in Dublin: Palmerston Road and Wellington Road, respectively. They can now be identified, in their proper ancestral lineage, as Dublin street preachers: Byrne was a sharply dressed confidant of the poor, while Larkin was their atheist sermonizer. Both men sometimes let themselves down, as they peddled utopian visions of the future. But they also had moments of greatness.

That spring, Larkin proposed that the Freedom of Dublin should be given to the playwright George Bernard Shaw, who had once recoiled in horror at the culture of censorship in Ireland. Larkin and Shaw were both autodidactic left-wing intellectuals. Shaw, like many Dublin writers, had needed to get away in order to find his voice. Leaving for good at the age of eighteen, he lived into his nineties, never lost his Dublin accent and once wrote, 'My sentimental regard for Ireland does not include the capital.'

Later that year, at the age of seventy-three, Larkin fell through a floor while carrying out an inspection of a union premises.[4] He suffered internal injuries but refused medical attention and was eventually admitted, against his will, to the Meath Hospital, where he died on 30 January 1947. His funeral was attended by hundreds of people, including Éamon de Valera and Alfie Byrne. The death of Larkin brought to an end a noble dogfight between two great ambassadors for the knackered, the bedraggled and the put-upon.

Between 22 January and 7 March of that year, the highest temperature recorded in the city of Dublin was five degrees Celsius. In the month of February, there were sixteen hours of sunshine.[5] It was the worst winter in living memory, and a bracing introduction to life in Ireland for J. P. Donleavy. The American writer remembered the snow piled high, the arctic cold and the dry warmth of Bewley's, before further exploration of the urban tundra.

In the better bars were clarets and burgundies, pickled onions, sausages, boiled eggs and sandwiches of ham, cheese and roast beef. But always on the very edges of these blessings lurked the cold desperate reality of the city . . . Begging for a penny or selling a newspaper, shoeless urchins, faces streaming phlegm, scattering across the grey glisteningly wet streets.[6]

Now in his mid-sixties, Byrne was no longer the crowd-pleasing showman of his heyday. Some of his ideas were met with guffaws (he once proposed a law to keep pedestrians walking on the left of footpaths) while others were simply ignored.[7] In March 1947, he made a crotchety attack on changes to Dáil procedure: 'We are not seeing democracy, but day after day we are getting nearer to dictatorship.'[8] On another occasion he demanded to know if the Minister for Agriculture 'intended to build up a reserve of tinned, preserved or frozen meat for human use'. When the Minister tried to bat him away, Byrne raised the spectre of milk and butter shortages. Exhausted by his scaremongering, the Ceann Comhairle asked him to leave the Dáil.[9] Undeterred, he tried to get the City Council to ban *Black Narcissus*, the classic Deborah Kerr film, because it caused 'pain and offence to many citizens'.[10]

Such crankiness was overlooked – or appreciated – by the voters of Dublin North-east. For the 1948 general election, Byrne paid the Emerald Girl Pipers' Band twelve pounds to march around the constituency in blue tartan kilts; he followed them everywhere in a horse-drawn brake. At the same time, local cinemas ran a slide before every movie: 'Alfie Byrne, T.D., will support any proposals to reduce the present excessive tax on cinema seats.'[11] Children also belted out a

Vote-for-Alfie song to the tune of McNamara's Band as they paraded the streets with his photograph hanging around their necks.[12]

> One name in dear Old Dublin,
> Well known to one and all,
> A name that has made history,
> In Dáil and City Hall.
> For close on half a century,
> If in trouble you would turn
> You always got loyal service
> From dear old Alfie Byrne.[13]

The lyrics were written by a supporter. Byrne paid twenty-three pounds to Monson, Robinson & Co. for the photographs and three banners, to be used by father and son, which afforded economies of scale, although Dad paid. The banners were not overburdened by wit:

- Byrne Does the Work
- We Want Alfie
- We Want Byrne
- Make Sure of Alfie First

Byrne was comfortably re-elected to the Dáil, and his son, Alfie Junior, regained the seat he had lost in 1944. 'Congratulations on a wonderful double,' wrote Alfie's brother Lar in a telegram. The national picture was less clear. Dev had been at the helm for sixteen years, longer than any other democratically elected leader in Europe. (Italian proverb: Governments are like underwear. They need to be changed often, for the same reason.) Six seats short of a majority, Fianna Fáil was unwilling to enter into a coalition. If the opposition parties formed one and secured the support of independents, *they* would be able to form a government. United by a desire to get de Valera out of office, Fine Gael, Labour, the new party Clann na Poblachta and smaller parties came together to create the first inter-party government.

Byrne played a small role in the toppling of Éamon de Valera. When it became clear that the Fine Gael leader, Richard Mulcahy, would not be acceptable as Taoiseach to Clann na Poblachta, Byrne and his son, Alfie Junior, were among a group of TDs who asked the Attorney General, John A. Costello, to assume the responsibility of heading the government. He hesitated. The Law Library was far more lucrative than Leinster House, and Costello worried that he might be a flop as Taoiseach but, eventually, he agreed.[14] After sixteen years, Fianna Fáil was finally deposed.

Later that year, during a press conference in Canada, John A. Costello surprised the world by declaring Ireland a republic. Byrne opposed this decision. Arguing that the country should remain a member of the Commonwealth, he said the declaration of a twenty-six-county republic was a slap in the face for anyone who still hoped to convince the people of Northern Ireland to join them in a single state. 'Instead of bringing a settlement of partition nearer they are pushing it further away,' he insisted. On another occasion he said, 'If we fail to remove the barrier of Partition, new movements, new parties, with new leaders will arise, in the years to come, and carry on the agitation.'[15] While that view was not widely supported by the public, Byrne received many letters from supporters of Fine Gael who felt betrayed. Among them was a former constituent now living in London:

We, in England, have obtained employment, which we were unable to do in Ireland, to feed our starving families . . . We also are aware that if the bill becomes law all the privileges which we now enjoy shall be stripped from us overnight . . . Would Mr Costello and his henchmen provide work and support and feed our wives and children? We very much doubt it . . . We would like you to inform the Costello Government that we in England are strongly opposed to any such action, and also that any hope of union with Northern Ireland is gone for ever.[16]

Byrne proposed that Ireland should remain a member of the Commonwealth, 'until the vast majority of the North who wanted goodwill and friendship with the people here, came in and helped us to help the world in its present chaotic conditions'.[17] But when other Commonwealth countries sent expressions of goodwill to the Irish government, Byrne withdrew his proposed amendment.[18]

In the summer of 1949, Byrne faced what a dramatist might call his central crisis: who was he, if not King Alfred; the Shaking Hand of Dublin; the Lord Mayor of Ireland? Tired of playing the emeritus role, and encouraged by the flatteries of the faithful, he tried to extend his record, by running for a tenth term as the Lord Mayor of Dublin. His son Alfie Junior was the only member to support his nomination. He got one vote.

That October, the government invited Byrne to represent Ireland at the British Commonwealth Relations Conference in Toronto. The Department of External Affairs urged him to remind the other delegates that Ireland was no longer a member of the Commonwealth. Byrne went one better. Enjoying his status as a Freeman of Toronto – a title conferred on his previous visit to North America – he spent ten days talking up Irish unity to anyone who would listen: taxi drivers, journalists and heads of state.

The 1950s is often depicted as a bleak period in modern Irish history, with high levels of emigration and unemployment. As a barker for the poor, Byrne told listeners of Radio Éireann about the masses 'left in their cheerless, fireless room or cottage gallantly trying to keep at bay the worst enemy of all – despair'.[19] The reality was more complex. It seemed as if the suburbs might finally be coming of age, served by new bus routes, churches and cinemas. Tim Carey has described this trinity – convenient transport, God and Clark Gable – as 'the three essential components of suburban living'.[20] The reader who remembers the opening of, say, the Casino cinema in Finglas can attest to the seismic effect of such a development.

In 1950, when the Minister for Health, Dr Noël Browne, tried to introduce free medical care for mothers and children up to the age of sixteen, stern opposition from doctors and the Catholic Church – who saw the plan as socialism – scuppered his plan. The crisis led to the demise of the inter-party government and, following the 1951 general election, Fianna Fáil formed a minority government with the support of independent TDs, including Browne.

Alfie Junior had been in poor health for two years. Despite being too ill to campaign in the 1951 election, his constituents returned him to the Dáil. And Alfie Senior was re-elected in Dublin North-east, where Fianna Fáil ran three candidates, with Oscar Traynor's surplus once again going to Harry Colley. (Charles J. Haughey was unsuccessful in the same constituency.) Later that year, the older Byrne again failed to be elected Lord Mayor. He got three votes. And when he ran for Leas Ceann Comhairle (deputy chair) of the Dáil, he was easily defeated by his Fianna Fáil opponent. One of the arguments made against him was the fact that he didn't speak Irish.

Seán T. O'Kelly was a more active president than Douglas Hyde. He travelled widely and made a determined effort to heal Civil War wounds. When O'Kelly was presented to the teams at an international football match, a spectator called out, 'Cut the grass and let's have a look at him.'[21] As O'Kelly's first term drew to a close, Byrne claimed that he had been asked to run for the presidency by five independent TDs.[22] Patrick Byrne remembers making a frantic late-night journey to Aughrim in Wicklow in search of political support for his father, but it was to no avail. Alfie Byrne ended up with seventeen of the twenty Dáil signatures that he needed to get on the ballot. Fine Gael declined to field a candidate, offering the barely credible official explanation that 'urgent political, economic and financial matters now require the exclusive attention of the people'. Seán T. O'Kelly was elected unopposed for a second term as the President of Ireland.

What was the real reason for Fine Gael's decision not to oppose O'Kelly? The leader of Fine Gael, Richard Mulcahy, was married to Min Ryan, whose sister, Phyllis, was married to President O'Kelly. The historian Charles Lysaght has hypothesized that Fine Gael allowed O'Kelly to stand unopposed because Mulcahy did not wish to keep his sister-in-law out of Áras an Uachtaráin.[23] On the other hand, Richard Mulcahy and Seán T. O'Kelly were said to despise each other. Patrick Maume has written that Mulcahy 'was never reconciled with O'Kelly, whom he publicly and privately spoke of with the utmost contempt'.[24]

Whatever the reason, Byrne lost out once again. It was his

third and final attempt to run for the presidency and, by the end of it, the Lord Mayor of Ireland must have known that he would never occupy a national office. In the 1930s, without belonging to a party, he had transcended the limits of being an independent politician. Now he had run up against those limits. Yet still Byrne refused to stop fighting.

In the summer of 1952, he ran for mayor yet again. This time, he secured the support of Fine Gael, but he lost out to Andrew Clarkin. Byrne was furious, telling the press that, half an hour before the meeting, he had been assured by two independents that they would propose and second him; both members subsequently voted against him.[25]

By this time, most of Alfie and Cissie's children had moved out, and the house on Palmerston Road felt too big. That summer, shortly after his parents moved into a smaller home on Upper Rathmines Road, Alfie Junior died of cancer.[26] He was thirty-nine years old. Byrne's feelings at the premature loss of his son and political protégé are not recorded, and the press focused only on the question of which of his sons would stand in the by-election in Dublin North-west.

Byrne decided that his son Tom would run; the other candidates were Clarkin, of Fianna Fáil, and Mick Fitzpatrick of Clann na Poblachta. Shortly before the by-election, Clarkin repeated a canard about Byrne: that he had supported the conscription of Irishmen in the First World War. 'This was a lie,' responded Byrne, 'and by resorting to such tactics Senator Clarkin was showing that he was in a panic, and realised that he would not be elected.'[27]

The leader of Fine Gael jumped to Byrne's defence. Richard Mulcahy wrote a caustic letter to Andrew Clarkin, demanding an apology to Byrne 'for the very slanderous and foul statement you made on 9 November'.[28] Mulcahy wrote that after the Rising, Byrne 'gave me unstinting help and comfort. Over many years he brought the same unstinting help and comfort to thousands of poor workers in the city of Dublin and caused them to honour and revere the position of Lord Mayor of their city – a position upon which your action in this matter has thrown a slur which should be removed.' In writing such a supportive letter, it is possible that Mulcahy was atoning for his decision not to nominate Byrne for the presidency.

Stakes duly raised, the *Irish Press* reported on an emotionally charged by-election:

> During the afternoon Gardaí dispersed a crowd of about 100 children who gathered outside St. Finbar's [National School] chanting 'We want Alfie.' [They] pelted Fianna Fáil cars with sods and tore down Fianna Fáil election placards erected outside the polling booth. Alderman A. Byrne, TD, was present during the incident.[29]

Tom Byrne was elected to the Dáil on the first count with 13,078 votes, which was almost double the Fianna Fáil vote.[30] Alfie introduced his son to the Dáil amid applause from the opposition benches.[31] Then he switched his attention to the Corporation, where Clarkin was unable to run for a third term as Lord Mayor, because his fellow councillors (mindful of Byrne's long reign in the 1930s) had decided that no one could hold the position for more than two consecutive terms. In the summer of 1953, Byrne ran against two other candidates – again, unsuccessfully.

He was seventy-one years old. There must have been times when all the palaver ('Can I depend on your support?') seemed beneath him. And younger rivals must have wondered why he bothered to run for Lord Mayor every year. Surely it was clear that he did not have enough support? The veteran speechifier was now as old as some of the buffers who had marvelled at the energy of 'the young iconoclast' in the House of Commons.[32] That was nearly forty years ago. Eventually, someone would have to ask the man himself. 'Alfie, when are you going to retire?'

The answer was never again.

17. Alfred X

Grow old along with me!
The best is yet to be,
The last of life, for which the first was made:
Our times are in his hand
Who saith, 'A whole I planned,
Youth shows but half; trust God: see all nor be afraid!'

Robert Browning

In May 1954, Alfie Byrne topped the poll in Dublin North-east. Fine Gael secured power in Leinster House, with John A. Costello becoming Taoiseach. But Byrne had another prize in sight. For the sixth year in a row, he decided to run for the post of Lord Mayor. On the day of the election, Maurice Dockrell of Fine Gael, knowing that he and his colleagues had no chance of getting their own man elected to the post, persuaded his fellow councillors to back the veteran independent.[1] And so, after a gap of fifteen years, Byrne was elected for a tenth term as Lord Mayor.

The *Irish Times* revealed the news with a photograph of a bowler hat and umbrella above the headline: 'Lord Mayor takes over.' Now seventy-two years old, Byrne did not move into the Mansion House. He stayed in Rathmines, where he had breakfast in bed at 10 a.m. before taking a number 12 bus into town. 'The conductor never took his bus-fare,' says Patrick Byrne. 'Alfie tried to pay but they wouldn't take his money. And the bus used to stop right outside the house, which was a hundred yards from the bus-stop.'

The first duty of the new Lord Mayor was to answer hundreds of letters and telegrams. Most expressed delight: 'Please accept hearty congratulations. The Mansion House is more like itself again now.'[2] Then came the hard-luck stories, the gifts and the stray enquiries. Many of the letters tell stories of penury and hardship, as they had in the 1930s, and begin or end with a request for a reference, a job, a house, some money or old clothes.[3] There was a letter from the Bell Brothers Circus, 'curious to know what would be the potential market for a real American circus'. Apparently, it had the best wild animal act in the world. 'Naturally, I am aware that this sort of thing is not within your realm of activities as a public servant . . . Would you be so kind, sir?'[4]

In his correspondence that year, Byrne shied away from articulating anything as coherent as a philosophy. However, as he moved towards the end of his rags-to-riches life, he often returned to the Victorian idea that work is its own reward. At its simplest: 'I like my work, and because I like it I never seem to tire.'[5] The tenth victory may have meant more than any other, because it spoke most eloquently to his patience and persistence; he comes across as proud in some of the letters, but never smug. There is courtesy, too, and quiet amusement. 'I am very sorry to have to tell you that Hopalong Cassidy has left Ireland and I am afraid that I do not know of his destination.'[6] When a woman from Beverly Hills sent the Lord Mayor of Dublin a bag of potatoes, he replied:

Thanks for the bag of potatoes. There was a difficulty about getting them in as there is an Agricultural Regulation which prohibits seed potatoes or vegetables of any kind coming into this country from other lands. I only mention this matter so that you will not go to the trouble of sending similar samples as expressions of goodwill to other parts of Ireland.[7]

Byrne remained a soft touch, even as he personally became more delicate. He could no longer hope to attend half a dozen functions in an evening, and he was too old, now, for the bicycle or even the auto-cycle. This was the elderly gentleman the younger man had pretended to be for years. 'Here's Alfie,' the urchins would shout as he gamely rounded a corner. On Grafton Street or St Stephen's Green, Alfred X would shake hands with a grave nod. The hat was still tipped to one and all. Tourists pointed, half-awed kids made fun of him, and on the rare occasions when he felt up to a miniature airshow of toffees or coins, the grush was distributed at a stately pace.

Byrne's assignments included meeting Rock Hudson on the set of the new Douglas Sirk movie, *Captain Lightfoot*, and opening an exhibition at the Royal Hibernian Academy.[8] On the way out of the exhibition, the Lord Mayor's coat could not be found in the cloakroom. The next morning, the artist Seán Keating dropped a note into the Mansion House, together with a dark grey overcoat. Keating apologized for 'any inconvenience caused you when I took your coat in mistake. I am glad to be able to say that I had the honour to wear it, if only by accident.'[9]

Dubliners who remember Alfie Byrne inevitably refer to the tail end of his forty-five-year career in public life. In the anecdotes of the city he appears as a venerable gent. The best of them demonstrate his compassion and his cuteness. For example, one day, Alfie Byrne was walking down the street with Denis Larkin, the son of Big Jim. A woman stopped Byrne for some money to buy food for her family. Byrne turned to Larkin and asked him for the loan of half a crown. Cornered into the deal, Larkin produced the money, and Byrne put it in the woman's palm, warmly urging her to enjoy a good meal. Around the corner, exactly the same thing happened, except this time Byrne produced half a crown from his own pocket. As they walked off, Larkin was fuming. 'The first time that happened, why did you have to borrow my money, when you could have used your own?' Byrne smiled and said, 'Yes, but that woman will now tell all her friends that Alfie Byrne went into debt on her behalf.'[10]

Byrne's colleagues on the City Council now included Charles J. Haughey, who had finished well down the field in Dublin North-east in the previous general election. Byrne corresponded with Haughey on leases for ex-servicemen.[11] A former lieutenant in the Local Defence Force, Haughey had considered an army career before deciding on politics, after qualifying as both an accountant and a barrister. He would learn a lot from the politics of Alfie Byrne, including how to buy the loyalty of constituents. It is arguable, indeed, that Charlie's turkeys at Christmas were a direct descendant of Alfie's lollipops all year round.

On 8 December 1954, the Tolka river burst its banks, damaging thousands of homes in Fairview, North Strand and Ballybough. This was the Lord Mayor's heartland, and the disaster required a dramatic response. Byrne reportedly got up from his sick bed in the middle of the night, first to inspect the scene, and then to organize a relief fund. His intervention was depicted as heroic in many obituaries, and it became the defining act of his tenth term. When the captain of an American naval ship tendered his sympathy 'to the civic authorities and to citizens of Dublin', Byrne told his secretary to notify the papers.[12] As usual, he was promoting himself and the downtrodden in the same breath. As he saw it, there was goodwill to be generated. The people needed cheering up. It would please them to know that powerful American men in boats were thinking about them.

But not everyone on the Tolka floodplain was impressed. In a sober account of the 1954 flooding, Eamon Dunphy wrote about how, as private tenants, his parents were unable to avail of the Corporation's relief services, and they 'despised' Alfie Byrne. 'In their view the sweets and the pennies were no substitute for proper representation, which this blueshirt publican never provided.' When Byrne appeared at the front gate, Dunphy's mother told him, 'Get out. There's nothing for you here.'[13]

Perhaps the most characteristic act in Byrne's tenth term as Lord Mayor was a short note to Fianna Fáil headquarters. Here are Alfie Byrne's final words to the people who tried to beat him for nearly thirty years:

Dear Mr Mullins,

I see that your Ard Fheis will be taking place [in the Round Room of the Mansion House] on 11th October. I hereby extend to you an invitation to use the halldoor of the Mayoral Residence and also the Drawingrooms and Diningrooms of the residence, for the reception of your important visitors and of my colleagues to the Feis.
 Kind regards,
Alfie Byrne, T.D.

Lord Mayor of Dublin

When Denis Gwynn bumped into the Lord Mayor in the middle of St Stephen's Green, the two men were walking to the same reception in Iveagh House. Gwynn observed his 'personal dignity, which was as impressive as his courage and independence of character', and sketched this flattering portrait of the mayor ('he never seemed to be in a rush, or even overworked') in his seventy-fourth year:

> Crowds were waiting outside to watch the many visitors arriving, and I saw Alfie Byrne walking slightly ahead of me, with his neatly rolled umbrella and black hat. There were delighted greetings from the crowd as he walked past, and he returned their salutation with perfect courtesy, and with none of the theatrical manner which politicians affect. A large car drew up, and bishops emerged in their robes while Alfie and I stood together at respectful distance. He had been at one ceremony after another through the day, besides performing his civic business, and he told me that he could not stay long at the reception because he had to attend another in Drogheda that same evening.[14]

Byrne's term was up on 4 July 1955. But he was not done yet: he decided to fight for re-election. His opponents were Bob Briscoe of Fianna Fáil and Denis Larkin of the Labour Party. When a councillor proposed that the position of Lord Mayor should rotate from party to party, 'as a position of honour given to one member of the Council for voluntary service to the city', Briscoe agreed, withdrawing his own name and announcing that Fianna Fáil would support the Labour candidate for Lord Mayor. Byrne was snookered. 'I heard this was going to happen last night,' he told the *Irish Times*. 'I was rung up from a Dublin public house and told it was going to happen.' Fianna Fáil and Labour offered feeble denials of collusion but, twelve months later, Bob Briscoe got his turn in the Mansion House.

On the morning after the election, Alfie Byrne was presented with an honorary Doctorate of Law from Trinity College, Dublin. Even after a lifetime of civic baubles, this was a signal achievement for a boy who left school at the age of thirteen to train as a bicycle mechanic across the road from Trinity College. Patrick Byrne says the presentation of that honorary degree was his father's proudest moment. It was also a repudiation of the Catholic definition of Irishness, for the clergy regarded Trinity as a notorious bastion of Protestantism. The Archbishop of Dublin, John Charles McQuaid, would not have been amused.[15]

At the ceremony, which was attended by colleagues, friends and scholars, Professor D. E. W. Wormell welcomed the honoree, 'who has held the office of Lord Mayor more frequently than any other man, whose name is linked all over the world with Dublin, a champion of the poor and needy, a friend of all men'.[16] The former barman received his doctorate from the Chancellor of the university, Rupert Edward Cecil Lee Guinness, the Earl of Iveagh. The other recipients of an honorary degree that afternoon included a professor of chemistry, a Polish philosopher and the head of clinical medicine at the University of Oxford. However, these erudite visitors were not fêted in the local press. Dublin wanted to read about Dr Alfie.

> There he sat, gloriously arrayed, like a taut figure in a stained glass window among the great academical figures of this city and our time, awaiting like a prizewinning boy his call to the rostrum for his prize. In clean-cut Latin he was called as Lord Mayor of Dublin, to listen to this eulogy and take

his scroll of honour, and the roar of cheering which carried him to the Chancellor's beneficent hands interpreted the feeling of a sentimental city.[17]

These homilies encourage us to imagine a graceful exit from public life. The following day, at a retirement dinner for city manager P. J. Hernon, tributes were also paid to Byrne, who wrote out a couplet of Browning on the menu in blue fountain pen: 'Grow old along with me!/The best is yet to be'.[18]

In January 1956, six months after his tenth term came to an end, Byrne was diagnosed with cancer of the oesophagus. 'Alfie was opened up,' recalls his son Patrick. 'But they didn't operate. It was too late.' In his pocket diary, the last appointment was made for 8 February. Two weeks later, he told the Dáil about the fate of some post office workers in Inchicore. 'They are not getting the same pay as similar men in private employment.' And the following day, Thursday 23 February, he asked a question about the supply of briquettes. It was the sort of inquiry he had made for over forty years. Like many others, it went unanswered.

On 13 March 1956, on the eve of his seventy-fourth birthday, Alderman Alfred Byrne TD died of pneumonia at his home on Rathmines Road. At the time of his death he was still a member of the Dáil and Dublin City Council. That afternoon, the Taoiseach, John A. Costello, interrupted proceedings in the Dáil to announce the news:

Deputy Byrne, or Alfie – as he was affectionately called by and known to the citizens of Dublin – was of a kind, courteous and most charitable disposition. He was probably the most popular representative we had in our capital city during the past fifty years. He had a personal charm that endeared him to all who had the pleasure of meeting him, and his old-world courtliness was known far and wide both at home and abroad. His constituents, and especially the poor of Dublin, will mourn his passing as that of a much-loved friend.

Costello went on to recall the highlights of Byrne's career, and made a point of saluting his 'sterling work on behalf of those executed after the Rising of 1916, as well as for the welfare of the political prisoners who were imprisoned at that time; indeed, his work in connection with the welfare of those imprisoned at that time is not so widely known as it ought to be'. At the end of the Taoiseach's speech, every deputy in the chamber stood to observe a short silence.

It was the largest funeral seen in the capital for many years. Most of the mourners were Dubliners, but in death, as in life, Byrne was hailed as the Lord Mayor of Ireland. Traffic in O'Connell Street was held up for twenty minutes to allow the cortège of over one hundred and fifty cars to pass, 'and at all the junctions along the route to Glasnevin people silently gathered to pay tribute to one of Dublin's most famous sons'.[19] Groups of women knelt in circles, saying the Rosary. One of the largest congregations was at the Five Lamps, where Byrne often made speeches during election campaigns. Flags flew at half mast all along the crowded route.

The President, Seán T. O'Kelly, did not attend the funeral. He was represented by his aide-de-camp. The government attendance in Glasnevin cemetery included the Tánaiste and seven Cabinet ministers. Éamon de Valera was among the politicians representing Fianna Fáil. After the crowds had dispersed, the *Manchester Guardian* noted that 'some elderly women stayed back to pray at the graveside for a man whose name will likely become a legend when the history of Dublin comes to be written'.[20]

The Byrne family received thousands of letters from strangers, and many eulogies were printed in the news-papers.[21] Flower-seller Rosie MacGrane left her usual pitch at St Stephen's Green to join one of the many groups from the poorer areas of Dublin who made a pilgrimage to the graveside. 'He always paid for my street licence,' she told the *People*. 'On his way to the Dáil he always got off his bike at my pitch and bought a bouquet which he gave to the first child he met.' Mary Byrne of Meath Street also brought flow-ers to the grave. 'Ten years ago I was being evicted,' she told the paper. 'My husband had died and I had eight children to bring up. I needed £2, so I wrote to Alfie. Two days later I got the receipt from the landlord.'[22]

The newspapers described a fierce advocate for the Easter rebels; a champion builder of bridges; the last real link with Westminster; a man who gave his vote and his seat to a woman; and a human wrecking-ball for the slums of Dublin. The *Irish Times* paid tribute to Byrne's popularity among the ordinary people of his native city:

> For more than forty years, he was a prominent figure in public life, serving his country and city with a rare and single-minded devotion. Himself a true Dubliner, he had a profound understanding of, and deep sympathy for, the needs and interests of his fellow-citizens, especially the poor. It is not too much to say that he lived for them, for wherever there was distress, he was promptly on the spot to ensure that assistance was made available with the utmost speed. His debonair, affable demeanour, his readiness at all

times to listen to those in search of help or advice, and his generosity to the poor made him one of the most popular personalities of our time.[23]

In a letter responding to that obituary, Thomas Bodkin, former director of the National Gallery of Ireland, wrote, 'I venture to suggest that steps should be taken immediately to inaugurate a fund for the purpose of erecting a statue to him. We do not have to wait for the verdict of history upon his merits. They are recognised by all who were privileged to know him.'

Epilogue: Whatever Happened to Alfie Byrne?

'No city exists in the present tense, it is the only
surviving mass-statement of our ancestors, and it
changes inversely to its inhabitants. It is old when
they are young, and when they grow old it has
become amazingly and shiningly young again.'

James Stephens[1]

This biography is published sixty-one years after the death of
Alfie Byrne. The Lord Mayor of Ireland is not mentioned in
the vast majority of books about Irish history. Even in David
Dickson's wonderful seven-hundred-page portrait of Dublin, he merits just one mention, in a footnote. Further, Byrne's
presence in the city is slight. There is some public housing
named after him, and a one-kilometre road between East
Wall and Clontarf. Until 2015, King Alfred was remembered
on that road with an ornate memorial throne. When it was
removed by Dublin City Council, the press mentioned vandalism and years of neglect.

Alfie Byrne was given the Freedom of Kilkenny and the
Freedom of Toronto, but not the Freedom of Dublin. His
great rival, Jim Larkin, is today remembered with a statue on
O'Connell Street; given his devotion to the poor of Dublin,
that seems fair. However, the prominence of Larkin – who
never once secured more votes than his rival – does raise a
pertinent question: Whatever happened to Alfie Byrne?

The subject of this book is an awkward presence in the republican account of modern Irish history. A constitutional nationalist who opposed the Easter Rising, Byrne never shut up about uniting Ireland. As a Home Rule MP, he found himself on the wrong side of history and, after the foundation of the Irish Free State, he refused to join another political party. When telling the story of Ireland, it is easy to overlook his contribution and inconvenient to shoehorn it into a history lesson. This is one explanation for his absence from the textbooks.

We must ask what, if anything, his story adds to our understanding of Irish history. Byrne had a remarkable life for many reasons, but he never attained high office at national level. He was not Taoiseach, Tánaiste or President, and he did not have a starring role in the birth of the Irish nation, like Michael Collins or Patrick Pearse.

Byrne was flawed. Indeed, the reader may conclude that he should be remembered, if at all, as an arch-populist who traded largesse for votes, leveraging his power to carve out a fiefdom in a part of Dublin that he abandoned as soon as his wealth allowed. An absent father, fond of censorship, he crushed free speech when it suited him, and he was, as Padraig Yeates said, the sort of politician who followed a mob 'to pick up a few votes'. He had several dubious allies, and then there was the jobbery. Byrne used his position as a public representative to benefit himself through the Sweepstakes and the Royal Liver. He often had more than one horse in the race.

There is also a legacy issue. Three of Byrne's sons became TDs. The last to enter politics, Patrick, took his late father's seat and retired unbeaten in 1969 after being elected four times in succession, itself a formidable achievement. But none of Byrne's grandchildren entered politics. The dynasty came to an end, and no one is there to claim the legacy. As a result, while many politicians inherited some of his traits, the pensioners of Dublin are more upfront about the debt. Many of them still cherish his memory.

Byrne's achievements primarily benefited a people and a city that remain neglected. Tension between the capital and the country was something he deplored. A man whose constituency once straddled both sides of the Liffey, he loved to bring citizens together, but in the years since his death the idea of Dublin has suffered, both outside the city and in its own imagination. The old boy in the bowler hat made people feel good about the capital. It is easy to be cynical about such claims until one sees what a great mayor can do for a place.

Byrne conspired in the idea that he was a jokey figure. It was part of the brand. An admirer once insisted that he was 'much more than a municipal comedian', but his appearance was old-fashioned and faintly comical – and he knew it.[2] Another contemporary said the Lord Mayor 'was perpetually conscious of the dignity of his office and studiously avoided familiarity himself, always addressing people as Mr, Mrs, or Miss or by military rank or title'. Yet he told everyone to call him Alfie. The style concealed the substance.

There are many reasons why Byrne has been forgotten by Official Ireland. The case for keeping his memory alive is shorter, and it starts with a unique bond: for thirty years, he was one of the most popular men in the state. In twenty-six public elections, he was elected twenty-five times. No one spent longer in the Mansion House; no one else served as an

MP, a TD, a Senator, a Councillor and the Lord Mayor of Dublin.

In addition to all those political victories, there is also the manner in which he played the game. Éamon de Valera said of himself that he only had to look into his own heart to know how the Irish people felt. This claim deserves an asterisk, because Byrne was closer to Dublin opinion, and his record-breaking life invites us to reconsider values like courtesy, tenacity and pride of place, all of which he embodied in a long career of extraordinary public service.

Byrne was a Home Rule dinosaur but, in some ways, he seems a remarkably modern figure. Promoting civic pride, he understood the power of social capital before the term existed. The tourist board asked for his help to promote Ireland because he was a master marketer who had already made his name in London and New York. He supported equal pay for women and spoke out about the treatment of children in industrial schools. His belief in persuasion as the only way to unite Ireland prefigured the Good Friday Agreement by seventy years. And finally, he gave many of the most marginalized men and women in Irish society a reason to believe in the future.

Alfie Byrne regarded it as a privilege to live in Dublin and, because of that, he devoted his life to furthering its ambitions. Transcending class and geography, he gave sweets to children and hope to everyone else: not to be poor. To be heard. To be proud. At a time when cynicism about politics has blinded many of us to the possibility that an individual can advance the human good, his story still has the capacity to inspire.

The subject of this book was a Dubliner whose charm, style and essential decency won admirers all over the world.

In giving his city a voice, he made the place smaller and more intimate, but also larger and more inclusive, and at his very best he encouraged a broader understanding of what it meant to be Irish. These are among the reasons why Alfie Byrne deserves to be remembered.

Appendix: The Lord Mayors of Dublin, 1900–2017

Year	Name	Party
1901–4	Timothy Harrington	United Irish League
1904–6	Joseph Hutchinson	United Irish League
1906–8	Joseph Patrick Nannetti	United Irish League
1908–9	Gerald O'Reilly	Nationalist
1909–10	William Coffey	Nationalist
1910–11	Michael Doyle	Nationalist
1911–12	John J. Farrell	Nationalist
1912–15	Lorcan Sherlock	Nationalist
1915–17	Sir James Gallagher	Independent
1917–20	Laurence O'Neill	Independent
1920–21	Thomas Kelly	Sinn Féin
1921–4	Laurence O'Neill	Independent
1924–30	*Position suspended*	
1930–39	Alfie Byrne	Independent
1939–41	Kathleen Clarke	Fianna Fáil
1941–3	Peadar Doyle	Fine Gael
1943–5	Martin O'Sullivan	Labour Party
1945–6	Peadar Doyle	Fine Gael
1946–7	John McCann	Fianna Fáil
1947–8	Patrick Cahill	Fine Gael
1948–9	John Breen	Labour Party
1949–50	Cormac Breathnach	Fianna Fáil
1950–51	Jack Belton	Fine Gael
1951–3	Andrew Clarkin	Fianna Fáil
1953–4	Bernard Butler	Fianna Fáil
1954–5	Alfie Byrne	Independent
1955–6	Denis Larkin	Labour Party
1956–7	Robert Briscoe	Fianna Fáil
1957–8	James Carroll	Independent
1958–9	Catherine Byrne	Fine Gael

1959–60	Philip Brady	Fianna Fáil
1960–61	Maurice E. Dockrell	Fine Gael
1961–2	Robert Briscoe	Fianna Fáil
1962–3	James O'Keeffe	Fine Gael
1963–4	Seán Moore	Fianna Fáil
1964–5	John McCann	Fianna Fáil
1965–7	Eugene Timmons	Fianna Fáil
1967–8	Thomas Stafford	Fianna Fáil
1968–9	Frank Cluskey	Labour Party
1969–74	*Position suspended*	
1974–5	James O'Keeffe	Fine Gael
1975–6	Paddy Dunne	Labour Party
1976–7	Jim Mitchell	Fine Gael
1977–8	Michael Collins	Labour Party
1978–9	Paddy Belton	Fine Gael
1979–80	William Cumiskey	Labour Party
1980–81	Fergus O'Brien	Fine Gael
1981–2	Alexis FitzGerald, Jr	Fine Gael
1982–3	Daniel Browne	Labour Party
1983–4	Michael Keating	Fine Gael
1984–5	Michael O'Halloran	Labour Party
1985–6	Jim Tunney	Fianna Fáil
1986–7	Bertie Ahern	Fianna Fáil
1987–8	Carmencita Hederman	Independent
1988–9	Ben Briscoe	Fianna Fáil
1989–90	Seán Haughey	Fianna Fáil
1990–91	Michael Donnelly	Fianna Fáil
1991–2	Seán Kenny	Labour Party
1992–3	Gay Mitchell	Fine Gael
1993–4	Tomás Mac Giolla	Workers' Party
1994–5	John Gormley	Green Party
1995–6	Seán D. Loftus	Independent
1996–7	Brendan Lynch	Independent
1997–8	John Stafford	Fianna Fáil
1998–9	Joe Doyle	Fine Gael
1999–2000	Mary Freehill	Labour Party

2000–2001	Maurice Ahern	Fianna Fáil
2001–2	Michael Mulcahy	Fianna Fáil
2002–3	Dermot Lacey	Labour Party
2003–4	Royston Brady	Fianna Fáil
2004–5	Michael Conaghan	Labour Party
2005–6	Catherine Byrne	Fine Gael
2006–7	Vincent Jackson	Independent
2007–8	Paddy Bourke	Labour Party
2008–9	Eibhlin Byrne	Fianna Fáil
2009–10	Emer Costello	Labour Party
2010–11	Gerry Breen	Fine Gael
2011–12	Andrew Montague	Labour Party
2012–13	Naoise Ó Muirí	Fine Gael
2013–14	Oisín Quinn	Labour Party
2014–15	Christy Burke	Independent
2015–16	Críona Ní Dhálaigh	Sinn Féin
2016–17	Brendan Carr	Labour Party
2017–18	Míchéal MacDonncha	Sinn Féin

Appendix: The Truth about Alfie Byrne and Batman

Several Dubliners have assured this author that the character of Alfred Pennyworth, Batman's butler, was based on Alfie Byrne. Experts are not convinced. One of them, Glen Weldon, says that Alfred started off as a portly major-domo, 'and it wasn't until the 1943 serial that Jerry Robinson tweaked his design to resemble that of actor William Austin'. Dr Will Brooker, who wrote *Batman Unmasked*, said, 'A butler is quite different from a Lord Mayor, and I believe Alfred is always coded as English . . . [I am] cautious about linking Alfred the butler with this real-life figure.'

Alfred Pennyworth may not be Alfie Byrne. However, there are striking similarities between Byrne and Batman, two comic-book heroes in the urban imagination. It is not, perhaps, the butler whom the mayor most closely resembles, but the caped crusader himself.

Alfie Byrne created a legend, in the process enabling Dublin to see itself as a larger, more generous place. In this account, the grey metropolis was not a boil on the edge of a small island, but a battleground in the war between good and evil. And Byrne was, of course, the hero of the story. A tireless fighter of red tape, red politics and blue movies, the Lord Mayor would keep the city safe from dangerous foreign influences. He was first on the scene of every disaster, and his fame was enlarged by the admiration of local schoolchildren, impressed by the speed at which he threw himself at Dublin. In the public imagination, Alfie Byrne was like Batman in a bowler hat.

Remember, too, that Batman has more than one identity. In Gotham, he is Bruce Wayne, the philanthropist businessman who is never out of the newspapers. After a tough childhood, he trains himself to defend the city; to do so, he creates a larger-than-life persona. Everyone knows that he has no real family life, because he is too busy saving people from cruel and irrational forces. His enemies wonder why he needs to wear that silly costume, but sometimes nothing else will do. Ultimately, we look up to Batman because he makes us believe in the possibility of a solution to our problems. There may still be a happy ending.

Alfred Pennyworth is the dapper, hard-working butler whose manners are reminiscent of an earlier age. Bruce Wayne was named after Robert the Bruce, but no one really knows how Bob Kane and Bill Finger chose the name of their butler. However, we do know that the two men who created Batman were living in New York in the spring of 1935. It is possible that they missed the much-hyped arrival of a short, dapper gentleman called Alfred Byrne. A few years later, they created a short, dapper gentleman called Alfred. This is why some Dubliners insist that Alfred in Batman *must* be based on Alfie Byrne. King Alfred. Alfred the Great.

The rumour is probably wrong, but it hardly matters, because every city needs its legends, and that is the truth about Alfie Byrne and Batman.

Acknowledgements

In 2012, Patrick Byrne donated his father's personal archive to the Little Museum of Dublin. There were six tea chests, totalling over four thousand artefacts, including diaries, invitations, opened and unopened letters, cards, Mass cards and nine large green leather-bound press books. An act of extraordinary generosity, that donation made this book possible.

Patrick's father is still remembered with affection by many older Dubliners. I often meet them in 'The Shaking Hand of Dublin', a permanent exhibition about Alfie Byrne in the Little Museum of Dublin. Some of those conversations were crucial to gaining a closer understanding of the subject, and I want to thank the hundreds of Dubliners whose insights and stories are dotted throughout the book. To record and share their memories is a privilege.

I am grateful to Bridget Hourican, Rhona Mahony, Michael Laffan, Catriona Crowe, Charles Lysaght, Martin O'Donoghue, Nicholas Sutton, Roland Budd, Christine Monk, Alan Fitzpatrick, Ed Brophy, Brian Geraghty, Roland Budd and Nicholas Sutton, for reading the manuscript and providing sound advice. David McEllin, who is writing a full-scale biography of Byrne that will become an invaluable work of reference, was extremely helpful; as someone with no real education, I am amazed by the kindness of serious scholars. I am also indebted to great historians such as Patrick Geoghegan, Padraig Yeates, Conor Mulvagh, Diarmaid Ferriter, Mike Cronin,

Anne Dolan, Fearghal McGarry, Ellen Rowley, R. F. Foster, Donal Fallon and Tommy Graham.

Turlough Galvin and Michael Byrne of Matheson, as well as Frank Callanan and Ernest Hanahoe, provided wise counsel around the 'Shaking Hand of Dublin' exhibition. Conversations with Michael O'Halloran, Adrienne O'Beirne, David Norris, Peter White, Mary Clark, Carmel Bolger, Fanchea Gibson, Elaine Byrne, Tricia Perrott, Liam Cosgrave, Declan Wallace, Conor Byrne, Mannix Flynn, Mary Freehill, Richard Belton, Lochlann Quinn, Winter Romanov Hynes, Dermot Lacey, Gerry Fay, June Anne Byrne and the late Adrian Hardiman provided me with valuable information about the subject of this book.

It is a privilege to work at the Little Museum of Dublin, and I salute our brilliant board, management, guides, volunteers, donors, supporters and members, as well as our patrons in Dublin City Council (I am particularly grateful to Owen Keegan, Declan Wallace and Michael Stubbs) and the Department of Arts, Heritage, Regional, Rural and Gaeltacht Affairs. The museum is a place of daily wonder, because it never worked on paper and cannot be contained.

In writing this book, I have been assisted by many colleagues, including Cory Egitton, Sarah Costigan, Kathryn McCance, Dylan Phillips, Eoin Bairead, Luke McManus, Suzanne Rourke, Ciaran Kinsella, Chantal Brown, Ronan Doheny, Edie Davis, Irina Fallon, Pauline Garde, Niamh Reynolds, Alan Roche, Natalie Williams, Sarah Thomas, Diarmuid Bolger, Sophie Andrews McCarroll, Karina Walsh, John Foyle, Fionnuala Maher and Jesse Carley. These people all deserve my thanks.

My agent, Robert Kirby, brought the idea for this book to my publisher, Michael McLoughlin of Penguin Ireland, and editor Brendan Barrington, who has spared me a great many blushes. Naturally, any mistakes in the text are entirely my own fault.

Some of this book was written in the Tyrone Guthrie Centre, Annamakerrig, a magical retreat for writers and artists in Newbliss, County Monaghan. I am also grateful to the staff of the Gilbert Archive, the National Library and the National Museum of Ireland, while the Royal Irish Academy must be congratulated for its magnificent *Dictionary of Irish Biography*. Karen Johnson, archivist at the Christian Brothers Province Centre, provided valuable assistance, and I could not have finished the book without access to the Irish Newspaper Archives, a fine online resource.

Finally, I am married to an extraordinary woman called Susan Jane White, who cooks things which have no right to be that delicious. Benjamin and Marty, you are the children who force your mother to have the occasional glass of biodynamic white wine. Please keep misbehaving.

Notes

The letters ABC refer to the Alfie Byrne Collection, personal documents and effects donated to the Little Museum of Dublin by the Byrne family.

1. Not to be Poor

1 Seán O'Casey, *Autobiographies II*, Faber & Faber, 1992, p. 38.
2 *Sunday Chronicle*, 22/8/1937.
3 Seán O'Casey, *Autobiographies II*, op. cit., p. 38.
4 *Irish Press*, 4/9/1943.
5 *Sunday Chronicle*, 22/8/1937.
6 *Sunday Chronicle*, 17/12/1934.
7 The letter to the *Irish Independent* is quoted in Eunan O'Halpin's *Dictionary of Irish Biography* entry on W. T. Cosgrave. O'Halpin says the letter 'shows a side of Cosgrave which his later career as a sober and steady statesman tended to obscure, his early radicalism and his antagonism towards Britain as the source of Ireland's woes'.
8 Quoted in Keith Jeffery (ed.), *An Irish Empire?: Aspects of Ireland and the British Empire*, Manchester University Press, 1996, p. 96.
9 'Each morning he rose at five for by six o'clock the dockside pubs were open.' *Alfie Byrne: Legendary Lord Mayor of Dublin*, unpublished lecture by David McEllin, Little Museum of Dublin, 15/5/2013.
10 *Sunday Chronicle*, 22/8/1937.
11 Letter from Mary Louise Cullen (née Leahy) sent 17 March 1955. In the same letter Cullen writes, 'My father, William

Leahy, you may recall was accidentally shot during the 1916 Troubles.' Thanking Cullen for her 'reminder of the old days', Byrne sent one pound to support the construction of 'a Lady Altar in our little church' in the town of Trowbridge, Wiltshire.

12 R. F. Foster, *Vivid Faces, The Revolutionary Generation in Ireland, 1890–1923*, Penguin, 2015, p. 2.

13 Dublin was notorious for high levels of public drunkenness and the attendant disorder, although the battle between the purveyors of alcohol and virtuous abstainers had its roots in much earlier struggles. When Arthur Edward Guinness, the man who gave St Stephen's Green to Dublin, was found guilty of bribing his way into parliament in 1868, his chief antagonist was Sir Dominic Corrigan, the heart surgeon and temperance campaigner.

14 These worlds are documented with great style in R. F. Foster's group portrait, *Vivid Faces*, op. cit.

15 In 1954, John Kelly wrote to Byrne from Eugene, Oregon, 'Not many of the old Strandville boys left. Remember me to Oscar Traynor.' The Lord Mayor responded, 'It is nice to be reminded of the old Strandville days.' Strandville and St Barnabas were two local soccer clubs – both played in Fairview Park. Alfie Byrne Collection: ABC.

16 *Sunday Chronicle*, 22/8/1937.

17 *Tipperary Star*, 14/9/1937. ABC.

18 *Freeman's Journal*, 10/1/1911.

2. The Alderman

1 Alderman Thomas Kelly, *The Streets of Dublin, 1910–1911*, Dublin Civic Trust, 2013, p. 142.

2 Undated note written by Byrne on City Hall Members Room notepaper.

3 *Lockout: Dublin 1913*, by Padraig Yeates, Gill & Macmillan, 2000, p. 120.

4 In correspondence with the author, 3/8/2016.

5 Kee and Lyons are quoted in *James Larkin: Lion of the Fold*, edited by Donal Nevin, Gill & Macmillan, 1998, pp. 383–4.

6 Padraig Yeates, *Lockout: Dublin 1913*, op. cit., p. 574.

7 Fionnuala Waldron, 'Defending the Cause: Parnell and the Drink Interest', in *Parnell Reconsidered*, edited by Pauric Travers and Donal McCartney, University College Dublin Press, 2013, p. 125.

8 Padraig Yeates, *Lockout: Dublin 1913*, op. cit., p. 574.

9 Ibid.

10 Book review by Benjamin Schwarz, 'Was the Great War Necessary?', *Atlantic Monthly*, May 1999.

11 Thomas Bartlett, *Ireland: A History*, Cambridge University Press, 2010, p. 374.

12 Michael Laffan, *Judging W. T. Cosgrave*, Royal Irish Academy, 2014, p. 51.

13 *Irish Independent*, 29/7/1914. This information was uncovered by Brian Hanley when he was historian-in-residence at Dublin City Library and Archive.

14 George Kearns and Patrick Maguire, *A to Z of All Old Dublin Cinemas*, self-published, 2006, p. 179.

3. Mr Byrne Goes to London

1 *Irish Times*, 8/9/1915.

2 Apparently, the two journalists who convinced Byrne to run for election as an MP were Michael Linnane and Bertie McRory. Linnane was a heavy-drinking pressman who also reported on

the sinking of the *Lusitania* in 1915. In *North of the Liffey: A Character Sketchbook*, Lenhar, 1984, Bernard Neary claimed that Linnane and McRory offered to write Byrne's election speeches.

3 Speaking on Dublin City FM, 5/1/2015, David McEllin said, 'Alfie wasn't formally nominated as an Irish Parliamentary Party candidate; none of the three [candidates] were; but he did become a member of the Irish Parliamentary Party at the time.'

4 *Irish Times*, 1/10/1915.

5 *Irish Times*, 2/10/1915.

6 *Irish Times*, 1/2/1932.

7 In the *Dictionary of Irish Biography*, Michael Laffan writes, 'With slight exaggeration [Redmond] would later boast that he took his seat, made his maiden speech, and was expelled from the House of Commons, all on the same evening.'

8 Speeches made in the House of Commons are from Hansard, except where stated.

9 *Irish Times*, 14/10/1915.

10 'Alfie Byrne: Legendary Lord Mayor of Dublin', unpublished lecture by David McEllin, Little Museum of Dublin, 15/5/2013

11 Austen Lake, writing in the *Boston Evening Transcript*, undated (1930s). ABC.

12 Ibid.

13 Damien Corless, *You'll Ruin Your Dinner*, Hachette Ireland, 2012, p. 13. Also, in Monsignor Michael J. Curran's witness statement to the Bureau of Military History, he said, 'The first victim was Noblett's sweetshop.'

14 *Church of Ireland Gazette*, 12/9/1937.

15 For many years, Byrne used the Collins quote on his election literature. The author has not seen the original of this letter from Collins, which was passed down through the Byrne family. Its whereabouts are unknown.

16 Bureau of Military History, witness statement by Frank Robbins, p. 101.

17 Fearghal McGarry, 'Helena Molony: A Revolutionary Life', *History Ireland* magazine, Vol. 21, No. 4.

18 Letter from Helena Molony to Byrne, 2/10/1952, ABC.

19 'After individual cross-examinations which lasted into the last afternoon—you came over to us and proposed tea, within the precincts, on the Terrace, I think. Then you said we had been confined for months and might like a sight of the open city, and proposed you should take us to some good restaurant where we would hear some music and have a nice afternoon tea. The wardresses were surprised at such an invitation (as well they might!) and gladly consented to the plan . . . we were still wearing the outdoor clothes we had been taken in. We often afterwards recalled the draggle-tailed shabby female tramps we must have appeared . . .' Letter to Byrne from Helena Molony. 2/10/1952, ABC.

20 Anne Marreco, *The Rebel Countess: The Life and Times of Constance Markievicz*, Phoenix Press, 1969, p. 233.

21 Letter from Helena Molony to Byrne, 2/10/1952. ABC.

22 'In the course of this interview someone had asked him if he would bring a letter home for a prisoner, but he deprecated the suggestion that he should dream of conniving at such a breach of the prison regulations. However, in an aside whisper, he conveyed the suggestion that if a note were placed surreptitiously in the tail pocket of his coat, he could not know about it till afterwards. The hint was taken, and the tail pocket was so stuffed with hastily written notes as to make an obvious bulge, while Byrne stalked majestically towards the gate. Every one of these notes was duly posted in Dublin, or in some cases, delivered in person.' Colonel Joseph V. Lawless, 'Recollections of the Anglo-Irish War: 1915–1921', Bureau of Military History.

23 R. F. Foster, *Vivid Faces*, Penguin, 2015, p. 138.

24 Barbara Dawson, introduction to the exhibition catalogue *Passion and Politics, Sir John Lavery: The Salon Revisited*. Dawson is director of Dublin City Gallery The Hugh Lane, which, as the Hugh Lane Gallery, was formally opened by Alfie Byrne on 19 June 1933. 'High Treason' is now on long-term loan to the Honorable Society of King's Inns from the British government's art collection.

25 *Sunday Chronicle*, 19/9/1937. Byrne kept a pamphlet, 'Passages taken from the manuscript written by Roger Casement in the condemned cell at Pentonville Prison', among his personal possessions until the end of his life. In it, Casement wrote, 'It is a strange strange fate, and now as I stand face to face with death I feel just as if they were going to kill a boy. For I feel like a boy – and my hands so free from blood and my heart always so compassionate and pitiful that I cannot comprehend how anyone wants to hang me.' ABC.

26 Con O'Leary, 'Poor Man's Friend: The Story of Dublin's Lord Mayor', *Sunday Graphic and Sunday News*, 18/11/1934. ABC.

27 *Freeman's Journal*, 16/7/1917. ABC.

28 On page 223 of *The Long Gestation* (St Martin's Press, 1999), Patrick Maume claimed that Byrne was offered a Sinn Féin nomination.

29 *Irish Independent*, 18/8/1937.

30 Letter to Senator Owen Sheehy Skeffington, 26/11/1954. ABC.

4. Free State Politician

1 'We all had our work cut out in that Ward, for it was the biggest industrial area in Dublin, composed mainly of the ex-British soldier element, whose wives looked on Alfie Byrne

as a tin god.' Thomas Leahy, witness statement to the Bureau of Military History, W.S. 660.

2 *Saturday Herald*, 17/1/1920.

3 The other men were James Newman Junior, William L'Estrange, John Kavanagh, James Higgins and Bernard Leavy. ABC.

4 Letter from Austin P. Kelly, 7/7/1954. ABC.

5 *Evening Herald*, 26/6/1922.

6 *Evening Herald*, 26/6/1922.

7 *Evening Mail*, 10/6/1941.

8 *Freeman's Journal*, 7/11/1922.

9 'The Intimate Story of Alfie Byrne', unknown newspaper, 12/9/1937.

10 Diarmaid Ferriter, *The Transformation of Ireland: 1900–2000*, Profile Books, 2004, p. 256.

11 *Alfie Byrne: Legendary Lord Mayor of Dublin*, unpublished lecture by David McEllin, Little Museum of Dublin, 15/5/2013.

12 Tim Carey, *Dublin since 1922*, Hachette Books, 2016, pp. 7, 59.

13 Undated letter to Byrne from a woman living in Summerhill. ABC.

14 *Southern Star*, 23/12/1922. In *Dublin since 1922*, op. cit. Tim Carey wrote, 'No matter how important the seat of state power might be, the state [had] little money to spend on it.'

15 *Sunday Independent*, 12/6/1927.

16 Letter from C. Dorney, 8, Seville Place, 21/8/1927.

17 When his old Irish Party colleague, Joseph Devlin, was elected a Member of Parliament for West Belfast in 1925, Byrne sent a telegram: 'Dublin friends delighted on your magnificent win, and congratulate Belfast on securing you as their representative when Dublin failed. Next step unity, North and South.' *Cork Examiner*, 7/4/1925. ABC.

18 *Irish Independent*, 17/5/1928.

19 Letter to Byrne from M. Harrington of the *Cork Examiner*, 14/10/1927. ABC. Even with the Corporation suspended,

dozens of people came to Byrne looking for one of the new houses in Drumcondra. 'I am living under very bad conditions at present,' explained one man. 'Myself, wife and three children are living [on Wharf Road] with my mother in law who has seven in family. That makes twelve of us living in two small bedrooms and small kitchen.'

20 Interview with Patrick Byrne, 9/11/2016.

21 *Donegal News*, 20/9/1930.

22 *Cork Examiner*, 2/10/1930.

23 *Roscommon Herald*, 18/10/1930.

24 *People*, 1/2/1931.

25 The office of alderman no longer exists. In 2017, the author asked Councillor Dermot Lacey – a former Lord Mayor of Dublin – if there was any chance that the office might be reinstated. He said, 'None.'

5. The Pied Piper of Dawson Street

1 *Daily Express*, 7/7/1931.

2 *Sunday Express*, 5/3/1961.

3 *Irish Independent*, 8/11/1930.

4 Letter to Byrne from Timothy P. Butler, 15/10/1954. Like Byrne, Butler had once been a pupil at the O'Connell School.

5 *Evening Mail*, 25/11/1930 ABC.

6 Tim Carey, *Dublin since 1922*, Hachette, 2016, p. 171.

7 'Old Friends are Best'. Election literature, 1940s. ABC.

8 *Waterford Star*, 28/9/1935. Sometimes the tone was more plodding. 'How long will Alfie Byrne be able to continue this shake-hands racket? Every hour of his every day is occupied with some sort of a public function, and the physical strain must be great indeed.'

9 Letter to Etta K. Fernelius, 14/2/1955.

10 'He has often dismissed the car after arriving at a public function so that I might be able to get home early. And then when the ceremony was over he would return to the Mansion House by tramcar.' *People*, 1/2/1931.

11 'Old Friends are Best'. Election literature, 1940s. ABC.

12 In response to this question in the Dáil, on 10 March 1926, Ernest Blythe said, 'The demand for cricket facilities was not found to be sufficient to justify the maintenance of the enclosure referred to and the surrounding fence.' Eventually, Byrne got his way.

13 *Irish Independent*, 28/11/1930.

14 *Sunday Express*, 5/3/1961.

15 *Irish Times*, 8/12/1930.

16 *Irish Times*, 9/12/1930.

17 *Drogheda Argus*, 13/12/1930.

18 *Dublin Letter*, unknown newspaper, 29/12/1930, ABC. 'A list of the functions at which he has presided, or assisted, would reveal remarkable variety bearing, however, the common stamp of beneficence. He is indefatigable in well-doing and courtesies, and it consorts with his temperament that they should revive ceremonial tending to civic dignity, as when he recently appeared in public attended by mace bearer and sword bearer.'

19 *Sunday Express*, 5/3/1961.

20 *Evening Mail*, 7/9/1931.

21 *Irish Independent*, 25/11/1931.

22 *Irish Times*, 16/1/1931.

23 *Tipperary Star*, 14/9/1937.

24 Byrne often complained about constituents who had to choose between buying the necessities and paying the rent. *Irish Times*, 16/1/1931.

25 *People,* 1/2/1931.

26 *Irish Times,* 13/2/1931.

27 *Daily Express,* 5/10/1938.

28 *Cork Examiner,* 17/6/1931.

29 *Irish Press,* 16/5/1931.

30 Anne Dolan, entry on Alfie Byrne in the *Dictionary of Irish Biography.*

31 *Sunday Express,* 5/3/1961.

32 *Belfast Newsletter,* 4/7/1931.

33 Ibid.

6. The Bleeding-Heart Racket

1 David Dickson, *Dublin: The Making of a Capital City,* Profile Books, 2014, p. 418.

2 *Irish Independent,* 16/10/1931. Byrne's reference to the 'occupation of one room by two families of sixteen persons in a Dublin tenement' was made in the Dáil on 2 August 1927.

3 *Evening Herald,* 10/9/1931.

4 *Irish Independent,* 31/10/1931.

5 *Irish Press,* 3/11/1931.

6 Tim Carey, *Dublin since 1922,* Hachette, 2016, p. 62.

7 *Evening Herald,* 4/4/1932.

8 *Irish Times,* 3/10/1931. On the same day, the *Liberator* pointed out, 'English money is being loaned to towns in the Free State to carry out local schemes of housing.'

9 *Evening Herald,* 15/3/1956. See also *Sunday Dispatch,* 7/2/1937.

10 *Evening Herald,* 10/4/1920.

11 *Irish Times,* 4/12/1930.

12 *World Telegram,* 15/3/1935.

13 On the back of the February 1932 issue of the *Catholic Mind* there is a full-page ad for the Sweepstakes. ABC.

Ireland: The Autobiography, edited by John Bowman, Penguin
Ireland, 2016, p. 202.

15 *Cork Examiner*, 15/3/1932.

16 *Irish Independent*, 7/12/2003.

17 *Irish Times*, 6/12/2003.

18 Marie Coleman, 'A terrible danger to the Morals of the Country: The Irish Hospitals' Sweepstake in Great Britain 1930–87'.
Published in *Proceedings of the Royal Irish Academy*, Vol. 105C, No.
5 (2005), p. 219.

19 Ibid., p. 197.

20 *New York Times*, 14/3/1935. The National Maternity Hospital
was the first 'electrified' hospital in the state.

21 John Morgan & Sons operated out of 36 Dawson Street. This
is where the Mansion House sherry was bought on account for
many years. In 1950, Christy Hendrick wrote to Alderman
Byrne from Delaware, 'In my hurried preparations in leaving
Ireland I overlooked the fact that I would require references
from my former employers . . . I would deem it a great personal favour if you would let me have such a letter of
recommendation, as soon as possible.' ABC.

22 *Irish Independent*, 7/12/2003.

23 *Irish Times*, 5/6/1934.

24 John Ryan, *Remembering How We Stood*, Lilliput Press, 1975,
p. 49.

7. Nibbling Carrots and the Rise of Fianna Fáil

1 Handwritten note from Byrne to W. T. Cosgrave, dated 'Saturday'. ABC. Also, Martin O'Donoghue adds some context:
'The Crosbie family which owned the *Cork Examiner* had been

Home Rule supporters pre-1918. The paper still retained some loyalties to those from similar backgrounds.'

2 *Evening Mail*, 5/1/1932.

3 When the Archbishop of Dublin turned the first sod on the site of the high altar in Phoenix Park, the Lord Mayor pocketed a piece of the soil and posted it to his sister, May, a Dominican nun in Africa.

4 *Truth*, 24/2/1932.

5 Hennessy recovered, whispering to Cosgrave, 'Go on with your speech, I want to hear you.' *Fermanagh Herald*, 20/2/1932.

6 *Truth*, 24/2/1932.

7 *Derry Journal*, 19/2/1932.

8 *Evening Standard*, 16/3/1932.

9 *Drogheda Argus*, 5/3/1932.

10 *Evening Standard*, 16/3/1932.

11 *Cork Examiner*, 19/3/1936.

12 *Daily Mail*, 15/4/1932.

13 *Irish Press*, 8/6/1932.

14 *Evening Herald*, 4/4/1932.

15 *Irish Press*, 28/6/1932.

16 *Irish Independent*, 28/6/1932. In 1939, Lauri would attend the service in Rome at which Mary, Byrne's daughter, was made a Dominican nun. *Irish Independent*, 25/5/1939.

17 Brendan Sexton, *Ireland and the Crown, 1922–1936*, Irish Academic Press, 1989, 'The Governor-Generalship of the Irish Free State', p. 126.

18 *Morning Post*, 4/7/1932.

19 *Irish Times*, 27/6/1932.

20 Some time later, a functionary discovered that the Lord Mayor was entitled, 'by virtue of his ancient associated office as Lord High Admiral of the Port of Dublin', to a salute of twelve guns each time he returned to the city. Byrne told the *Daily Express*

that he had no intention of insisting on his right to the salute. (Yes, the idea must have tickled him.) The residents of Ringsend were doubtless relieved to hear of this position. One wag remarked, 'What good is a salute of twelve cannons to a man who this year entertained five cardinals and more than a score of bishops?'.

8. Dangerous Idiots

1 *Catholic Herald*, 10/9/1932.
2 Terence Brown, *Ireland: A Social and Cultural History, 1922 to the Present*, Cornell, 1981, p. 131.
3 George returned to Dublin some time later, and worked as a barber in Fairview for many years; the restaurant critic Tom Doorley remembers having his hair cut by the mayor's brother.
4 *Sunday Chronicle*, 3/10/1937.
5 *Irish Times*, 29/12/1932.
6 *Irish Press* 30/12/1932.
7 *Cork Examiner*, 30/12/1932.
8 Ciara Meehan, *The Cosgrave Party*, Royal Irish Academy, 2010, p. 215.
9 *Irish Times*, 2/1/1933.
10 *Cork Examiner*, 21/1/1933.
11 *Cork Examiner*, 24/10/1931.
12 *Ulster Herald*, 24/10/1931.
13 Diarmaid Ferriter, *The Transformation of Ireland: 1900–2000*, Profile Books, 2004, p. 416.
14 Election leaflet 'to wish you and the members of your household many blessings and happiness for the New Year, and to express the sincere hope that 1933 will be the beginning of a more prosperous period, in which all your troubles will soon be ended'. 12/1/1933. ABC.

15 *Irish Independent*, 25/1/1933. Byrne retired to bed but was soon back on his feet, according to the *Irish Times*: 'Alderman Byrne was roughly treated by some persons who were outside the Deverell Place polling station on Tuesday, and suffered a good deal of pain from a blow that he received. The Lord Mayor is, however, expected to be well enough to be about to-day.'

16 *Belfast Telegraph*, 24/1/1933. On polling day, the *Belfast Telegraph* noticed that several cars bringing voters to the booths had Ulster plates: 'Members of the A.C.A. were particularly active in Dublin throughout the day. Groups were on duty outside every polling booth, while others moved about in threes and fours in side streets where voters were being assisted by motorists to the polling stations.' Pathé News reported that Byrne was 'set upon by a young hooligan who promptly knocked [Byrne] down with a straight left. He said that he was fully aware of the dignity of his office but no Irishman could allow himself to be struck without retaliation.'

17 In correspondence with the author, Fearghal McGarry wrote that the photograph was probably taken in 1934. On 9 February of that year, the *Irish Times* reported on a United Ireland reception in the Mansion House: 'When General O'Duffy arrived, about eighteen hundred people had percolated into the hall . . . The vice-presidents – Mr Cosgrave, Mr MacDermot and Mr Dillon – received General O'Duffy in the drawing room, and they were joined by the Lord Mayor, who headed the procession to the Round Room through an archway of blue shirts.' Byrne's presence was supportive, certainly, although it was normal for the first citizen to welcome guests to events in the Mansion House. One of his last acts as mayor was to offer Fianna Fáil use of the facilities in the Mansion House for their upcoming Ard Fheis in the Round Room, and it was typical of the mayor to extend such hospitality. For

example, in June 1935 the *Belfast Newsletter* reported that at the Methodist Conference, Byrne 'was anxious that the visitors to the Mansion House should feel comfortable; so he put in an appearance prior to the public meeting. Moving freely among the conference delegates he bade them welcome with all his characteristic bonhomie.'

18 Yeates used this phrase in correspondence with the author, 3/8/2016.

19 Anne Dolan told this author that a challenge for anyone investigating the allegation that Alfie Byrne might have been anti-Semitic 'is the gap between what we would rightly perceive as anti-Semitism if it was uttered today and what seemed to be accepted in the rhetoric of the 1920s and 1930s. This is a considerable interpretative problem and one which scholars of this period have to grapple with by immersing themselves in the register of the language as it was perceived and understood at the time.' Padraig Yeates adds, 'I am old enough to remember Dubliners routinely referring to money lenders as "Jewmen", but the term did not literally mean that the person in question was Jewish or that the commentator was anti-Semitic.'

20 In correspondence with the author, Cronin also observed that Eoin O'Duffy 'went out of his way to distance the blueshirts from anti-Semitism and even met with the Chief Rabbi to ensure the Jewish community of good relations between the two groups'.

21 Byrne was absent from Dáil debates on the Non-intervention Bill on the Spanish Civil War in February 1937.

22 Letter to Byrne from Eoin O'Duffy, 30/12/1936. ABC.

23 Quoted in Pauric J. Dempsey's entry on Patrick Belton, *Dictionary of Irish Biography*, p. 446.

24 On 16 June 2016, Colum Kenny wrote an 'Irishman's Diary' on this subject in the *Irish Times*.

25 Isaac Herzog wrote to Byrne on 19 June 1936, in response to an appeal to religious leaders, to ask their followers to vote in the upcoming elections: 'My dear Lord Mayor, I heartily agree with what you say in your esteemed letter of the 16th inst. It is the bounden duty of all citizens to exercise their franchise and record their votes in municipal as well as in parliamentary elections. I shall certainly speak to people about this very important matter. Yours sincerely.' Other respondents to Byrne's appeal included Reverend Mills of the York Street Congregational Church and the Dean of St Patrick's Cathedral, David Ruddell Wilson. The text of the 1954 letter from Louis Elliman reads, 'On behalf of my co-Directors and myself may I congratulate you on your election to your accustomed position of First Citizen. Wishing you a very pleasant year of office and with kindest personal regards.'

26 *Irish Independent*, 4/11/1931; *Irish Independent*, 6/5/1932. In 1954, he forwarded a donation from an Irish-American Jewish woman to the Chief Rabbi, 33 Bloomfield Avenue, 'for the leading orthodox synagogue in Dublin'. ABC.

27 Letter from Byrne in response to invitation from Mrs J. Feldman, 26/11/1954. 'I shall have much pleasure in being present.' ABC.

9. How You Play the Game

1 *Offaly Chronicle*, 19/1/1933.

2 *Irish Times*, 1/3/1933.

3 *Irish Independent*, 2/3/1933.

4 *Evening Mail*, 17/6/1933.

5 *Evening Herald*, 16/1/1933; letter to Byrne from Dakota, General Printers & Carton Manufacturers, 26/4/1954, ABC; undated letter to Byrne from W. M. Nash in Bootle, Lancashire. ABC.

6 In correspondence with the author, 2016.

7 *Belfast Newsletter,* 18/10/1930.

8 The Lord Mayor wrote the word 'Envelopes' across the top of some of the begging letters he received: the sender was to be hired to stuff envelopes with campaign literature. In 1948, J. Butler from Mercer Street wrote to him, 'I take the liberty of writing to you as the elections is drawing near to know if you want any envelopes addressed or any work which would help, I have done some work for you in elections before . . . trust a satisfactory reply as I have a wife and nine children, I am unemployed, and every little helps in these hard times.'

9 *Northern Whig,* 26/6/1933.

10 Interview with Patrick Byrne, 9/11/2016.

11 *Evening Mail,* 17/6/1933.

12 *Irish Independent,* 28/10/1933.

13 *Daily Express,* 10/4/1939.

14 *Irish Times,* 2/11/1934. Another reporter said Byrne was 'a close friend from whom they expected nothing but the greatest kindliness and courtesy'.

15 Joyce was writing to his son, Giorgio, in New York. *Letters of James Joyce,* Vol. III, Richard Ellmann (ed.), 19/2/1935, p. 346.

16 Kevin Rockett, *Irish Film Censorship,* Four Courts Press, Dublin, 2004, p. 13. Montgomery insisted that films in which the following abominations were mentioned had to be edited or banned altogether: blasphemy, incest, divorce, contraception, abortion, homosexuality, adultery, illegitimacy. Disturbed by the appearance of short skirts, he once said of a film under review, 'The girl dancing on the village green shows more leg than I've seen on any village green in Ireland. Better amputate them.' Elsewhere, the banks of the Dodder have been used as a lovers' lane by generations of Dubliners. Montgomery once

said, 'The trees along the Dodder are more sinned against than sinning.' At least he had a sense of humour.

17 Anthony Cronin made this point in *Magnum Ireland*, Thames and Hudson, 2005, p. 17. Also, Diarmaid Ferriter has observed that 'elite debates about censorship or contraception were of little relevance to the majority, who carried on reading the Westerns and romances they desired and having the children they felt duty-bound to'. Diarmaid Ferriter, *The Transformation of Ireland: 1900–2000*, Profile Books, 2004, p. 361.

18 Letter to Byrne from a man who lived at 8 Inns Quay, 19/8/1927. ABC.

19 *Irish Press*, 19/11/1934.

20 *Irish Independent*, 20/11/1934.

21 *Irish Press*, 20/11/1934.

22 *Irish Times*, 4/12/1934.

23 *Irish Press*, 6/2/1934. There are very fine pieces about the anti-jazz movement by Donal Fallon on comeheretome.com and by Cathal Brennan on theirishstory.com.

24 *Daily Express*, 26/11/1934. The *Sunday Dispatch* also ridiculed his calls for more censorship: 'We are already unique among modern civilisations in having a Board of Literary Censors and the most severe film censorship. But this, apparently, is not enough. It has always seemed to me that so long as we have this censorship, and so long as the law makes it an offence to sell a book or show a film which has been banned by censors, then it should be equally an offence to attempt to prevent or otherwise interfere with the showing of a film or the production of a show which has not been so banned.'

25 *Derry Journal*, 3/12/1934.

10. Mission to America

1 *Letters of James Joyce*, Vol. III, Richard Ellmann (ed.), 19/2/1935, p. 346.

2 'But you've forgotten to ask me about one of our principal industries – the Irish sweepstakes. Through them we have erected one of the best hospital systems in the world, Germany and America included. We are now opening the finest maternity hospital in Europe, and many hospitals have been opened in various parts of Ireland through this fund' (*New York Times*, 14/3/1935). Later that month, he told another paper, the *New Era Lancaster*, 'The boundary question between the north and south of Ireland is still a barrier to peace, progress and happiness among our people. While that boundary exists there will be trouble among my countrymen.'

3 *Gazette and Daily*, 4/3/1935.

4 *Daily Mirror*, 15/3/1935.

5 *Evening Mail*, 5/4/1935.

6 Ibid.

7 'This morning I received an American newspaper which does not contain a single reference to or a photograph of the Lord Mayor of Dublin, although it is dated Sunday, March 31st – a time when the Lord Mayor was still touring that interesting country. This paper is a curiosity since it is probably the only American newspaper which has gone to press during recent months without some reference to the Lord Mayor.' *Evening Mail*, 16/4/1935.

8 *New Era Lancaster*, 4/3/1935.

9 *American*, 22/3/1935.

10 *Irish Times*, 2/4/1935.

11 *American*, 27/3/1935.

12 John Fitzgerald was John F. Kennedy's maternal grandfather. In 1938, Fitzgerald's son-in-law, Joseph Kennedy, would be formally welcomed to Dublin by Lord Mayor Alfie Byrne.

13 *Irish Independent*, 6/4/1935.

14 *Evening Herald*, 13/4/1935.

15 *Church of Ireland Gazette*, 3/10/1937.

16 *New York Daily Mirror*, 14/3/1935. Back in Dublin, a cartoon in *Dublin Opinion* had Byrne leaving America for the return to Europe. Walking up the gangplank of a ship, he extends a right hand to the officers onboard. Hundreds of admirers see him off. Each has their right hand bandaged in a sling. A cat, perched on the rooftop, has one paw in a sling. Even a clock on a skyscraper has its big hand bandaged.

17 'That was a wonderful idea of yours to get people to come to Ireland. So I have written a lyric, which I have enclosed'; Letter to H. Johnston, umbrella manufacturers. 'I shall be grateful if you will reply to the writer of the attached letter . . . he wishes to purchase a genuine Irish shillelagh.' ABC; *Evening Herald*, 7/6/1939.

18 Letter to Byrne from T. J. M Sheehy, Chief Officer, Press and Public Relations Department, Bord Failte, 22/2/1955. ABC.

19 In the 1970s, the youngest of Byrne's children, Sylvester Louis, was president of the Irish Travel Agents Association. His speciality was ecumenical tours of the Holy Land. Sylvester's son Conor, who is a CFO in Sydney, Australia, says, 'He was the first travel agent to do charter flights there. He'd get Protestant and Catholic bishops to come together on these diocesan pilgrimages.' Sylvester also sold Frank McCourt a one-way ticket to New York.

20 *Evening Mail*, 2/7/1935.

21 *Evening Herald*, 9/7/1935.

22 *Evening Mail*, 9/8/1935.

23 *Irish Press*, 18/9/1935.
24 *Daily Express*, 18/9/1935.

11. The Shaking Hand of Dublin

1 *Cork Examiner*, 11/1/1963.
2 Letter to Byrne from a man in Catherine's Lane, off North William Street, undated. ABC.
3 *Sunday Chronicle*, 22/8/1937.
4 *Daily Express*, 24/10/1935.
5 Appointments diary for the Lord Mayor, 16/11/1934. ABC.
6 *Evening Mail*, 25/8/1937. In 1953, Byrne was an advocate for padder tennis (think mini-tennis with bats instead of racquets) in public parks around the city. June Anne Byrne (née Fitzpatrick), who played in Junior Wimbledon at the age of seventeen, remembers Byrne in his morning suit, with a flower in his buttonhole, encouraging youngsters. 'If it wasn't for him,' she told this author, 'the kids wouldn't have come in to have a go.'
7 *Belfast Newsletter*, 5/11/1935.
8 *Sunday Dispatch*, 24/11/1935.
9 *Irish Times*, 5/12/1935.
10 *Longford Leader*, 28/12/1935.
11 *Sunday Chronicle*, 22/8/1937.
12 *Manchester Guardian*, 10/10/1933. ABC.
13 *People*, 12/10/1930.
14 *Evening Herald*, 14/12/1932.
15 *Irish Times*, 4/11/1932.
16 Tim Carey, *Dublin since 1922*, Hachette, 2016, p. 107.
17 Ellen Rowley, 'Housing the masses in 1930s Dublin and the position of Alfie Byrne'. Unpublished lecture, 30/10/2012, Gilbert Lectures, Dublin.

18 Diarmaid Ferriter, *The Transformation of Ireland: 1900–2000*, Profile Books, 2004, p. 407.

19 Typed draft of speech, undated. ABC.

20 *News Chronicle*, 3/2/1937. Byrne made this comment in his speech as guest of honour at a dinner for the Liverpool Wholesale Fresh Meat Trade Association.

21 Ellen Rowley, 'Housing the masses in 1930s Dublin and the position of Alfie Byrne', op. cit.

22 *Sunday Times*, 8/9/1935. 'Expert visitors have said that these new flats are as up-to-date as any in Great Britain or on the Continent.'

23 *Evening Mail*, 2/7/1938.

24 Bill Cullen, *It's a Long Way from Penny Apples*, Mercier Press, 2001, pp. 88–118.

25 Undated letter from Thomas O'Reilly. ABC.

26 *Irish Times*, 7/1/1936.

27 Letter to Byrne from M. Harrington, Dublin editor of the *Cork Examiner*, 14/10/1927. ABC.

28 London *Times*, 17/3/1939.

29 Letter from Dublin Corporation, 10/9/1948. ABC.

12. The Empire Mind and the Orchard Thieves

1 'Old Friends are Best'. Election literature, 1940s. ABC.

2 Ibid.

3 From the introduction to *Ireland: The Autobiography*, John Bowman (ed.), Penguin Ireland, 2016, p. xiv.

4 *Sunderland Echo*, 12/12/1934.

5 *Irish Press*, 5/1/1932.

6 Letter from Gerard Hand, 33 Chelmsford Road, dated 6 July, year unknown. ABC.

7 *Evening Herald*, 27/1/1936.

8 *Irish Independent*, 30/1/1936.

9 *Liverpool Post*, 6/2/1936.

10 Alfie Byrne election leaflet, 1948. 'A senior politician tried to incite the people against me by stating that I had "The Commonwealth Outlook".' ABC.

11 Letter from Byrne to the *Evening Mail*, 11/6/1936.

12 *Irish Times*, 6/6/1936.

13 In 1927, Byrne asked W. T. Cosgrave to introduce legislation to protect wild birds. Later, he chaired the first protest against the horse trade between Ireland and the continent. His interest in the subject was encouraged by angry constituents: 'Surely you, as Lord Mayor, could exert authority over your Corporation and Officials to put an end to this ever-recurring complaint of cruelty.' Letter to Byrne, 8/11/1954. ABC.

14 *Daily Express*, 27/7/1937.

15 *Derry People*, 3/6/1937.

16 *News Review*, 20/5/1937.

17 'So honoured,' wrote Jimmy O'Dea, 'but so improper for me to be first.' The bottom of some pages in the visitors' book feature the night-time scrawls of children, probably in pyjamas, standing on tippy-toe. We are asked to believe that the visitors included Mickey and Minnie Mouse from Goofyland. There is even a bit of sibling rivalry in the remarks column: 'Okay, except for Paddy.' In 2012, the same Patrick Byrne, who was the sixth child of Alfie and Cissie Byrne, donated his father's archive to the Little Museum of Dublin. There are over four thousand artefacts in the Alfie Byrne Collection, the primary source for this biography.

18 *Daily Express*, 29/6/1937.

19 *Evening Mail*, 5/7/1955.

20 Tom Garvin, 'Irish Voters and Irish Political Development: A Comparative Perspective', in *Economic and Social Review*, Vol. 8, No. 3, 1977, p. 179.

21 *People's Press*, 3/6/1937.

22 *Irish Times*, 3/6/1937.

23 Diarmaid Ferriter, *The Transformation of Ireland: 1900–2000*, Profile Books, 2004, p. 325.

24 Letter to Byrne from William P. Everard, 4/8/1926. ABC.

25 'Inquiries show that more than 30 children appeared in the juvenile court last Friday. Among the accusations were stone throwing, housebreaking, and robbing orchards. Their ages ranged from eight to eleven years. In several cases where previous offences were proved the children were sent to industrial schools for three years. When they were removed from the courtroom and put in a van to be taken away parents crowded around and the mothers wept.' *Daily Express*, 24/8/1937.

26 A conspiracy theorist might think it relevant that Edward J. Little's brother, P.J., was a Fianna Fáil TD.

27 *Irish Independent*, 20/8/1937.

28 *Catholic Herald*, 3/9/1937.

29 *Evening Mail*, 26/8/1937. Byrne was the subject of even more explicit criticism on the letters page of the same paper. One A. F. Doyle wrote: 'It will come as a shock to most observers of law and honesty, and especially those who spend their few spare hours and shillings to beautify their homes, to find the Lord Mayor of Dublin criticising the actions of one of our learned justices. It is idle to compare the recent depravations of "youths" with the schoolboy tactics of stealing a few handfuls of fruit for a "lark". When a band of men or youths enter a number of gardens and smash all before them, even when they do not take away their loot, it is a violation of God's law, and the moral code of any civilised community, and those who seek to minimise or condone it are little better than enemies of that code. Destruction and stealing of private or public property is either right or wrong; there can be no half

way house . . . There is little good in responsible heads of the city prating about civic spirit on the one hand, and attempting to condone vandalism on the other.'

30 *Irish Times*, 26/8/1937.

31 *Evening Herald*, 10/9/1937.

32 *Irish Independent*, 10/9/1937.

33 *Irish Independent*, 10/6/2009.

34 Letter to Byrne from a woman in Larkhill, 21/8/1954. ABC.

13. Alfie for President

1 Dermot Keogh, *Twentieth-century Ireland*, Gill & Macmillan, 2005, pp. 98, 103.

2 *Sunday Chronicle*, 22/8/1937.

3 *Midland Tribune*, 11/9/1937.

4 *Sunday Chronicle*, 26/9/1937.

5 *Tipperary Star*, 2/10/1937.

6 Unattributed and undated cutting from the Byrne archive. ABC.

7 *Daily Mail*, 18/12/1937.

8 *Daily Mirror*, 23/12/1937.

9 *Frontier Sentinel*, 15/1/1938.

10 *Irish Independent*, 10/2/1938.

11 *Evening Mail*, 11/2/1938.

12 *Daily Sketch*, 3/3/1938.

13 *Sunday Independent*, 14/4/1938.

14 This quotation has been put into the first person.

15 *Daily Express*, 23/4/1938.

16 *Birmingham Post*, 25/4/1938.

17 Declan Kiberd, 'Irish Literature and Irish History', in the *Oxford History of Ireland*, R. F. Foster (ed.), Oxford University Press, 2001, p. 268.

18 Quoted in Brian Murphy, *Forgotten Patriot: Douglas Hyde and the Foundation of the Irish Presidency*, The Collins Press, 2016, p. 14.

19 Letter to the *Irish Times* from A. M. Sullivan, a lawyer who had worked alongside Hyde in the Gaelic League. Quoted in ibid., p. 175.

20 They had known each other for years. For example, on 14 December 1934, Dr Hyde paid a visit to the Lord Mayor in the Mansion House. Earlier that year, Byrne led a campaign to pay a public tribute to Hyde for his great services to the Irish nation.

14. No More Shall We Hear of the Mansion House Rat

1 *Irish Times*, 2/7/1938.

2 *Strabane Chronicle*, 11/6/1938.

3 *Irish Press*, 28/6/1938.

4 *Irish Times*, 28/6/1938. ABC.

5 *Irish Press*, 28/6/1938.

6 *Irish Times*, 28/6/1938.

7 *Irish Press*, 9/9/1938.

8 *Irish Times*, 28/9/1938.

9 *Irish Times*, 16/1/1939.

10 *Irish Independent*, 16/1/1939.

11 *Evening Mail*, 8/5/1939.

12 *Yorkshire Evening News*, 25/5/1939.

13 *Irish Times*, 26/6/1939.

14 *Longford Leader*, 1/7/1939.

15 Ibid.

16 *Irish Independent*, 28/6/1939.

17 *Northern Whig*, 27/6/1939.

18 *Irish Press*, 27/6/1939.

19 *Cork Examiner,* 27/6/1939.

20 *Northern Whig,* 27/6/1939.

21 *Anglo Celt,* 1/7/1939.

22 *Northern Whig,* 27/6/1939.

23 *Longford Leader,* 1/7/1939.

24 This quotation has been put into the first person. The original quotation reads, 'He never seemed to forget that she represented a man whom all Ireland honoured. It was because she represented that man that she was being put in that chair.' *Irish Independent,* 1/7/1939.

25 *Irish Press,* 29/6/1939.

26 *Birmingham Mail,* 8/7/1939.

27 Helen Litton, 'Kathleen Clarke, First Woman Lord Mayor of Dublin', in *Leaders of the City: Dublin's First Citizens 1500–1950,* Ruth McManus and Lisa Marie Griffith (eds.), Four Courts Press, 2013, p. 171.

28 *Irish Press,* 28/7/1939.

29 *Evening Herald,* 28/6/1939.

30 Ibid.

31 Helen Litton, 'Kathleen Clarke, First Woman Lord Mayor of Dublin', op. cit.

32 *Irish Times,* 12/7/1939.

33 *Evening Mail,* 30/6/1939.

15. The Emergency

1 *Sunday Independent,* 2/7/1939.

2 Meanwhile, Cissie became more withdrawn. 'She was a retiring sort of person,' says their son Patrick. 'And she was more religious than Alfie.' In her later years, Mrs Byrne played the card game solo, as well as a weekly game of bridge, and was a regular at Mass.

3 Scholars such as Dr John Garvin and Janet E. Lewis have explored the connections between *Finnegans Wake* and real-life characters in Dublin. For example, see 'Some Irish and Anglo-Irish Allusions in *Finnegans Wake*', by Garvin, in *James Joyce Quarterly*, Vol. 11, No. 3 (spring, 1974), pp. 266–78.

4 Correspondence to Byrne from Munster and Leinster Bank, 1940. ABC.

5 *Longford Leader*, 19/8/1939.

6 *Irish Press*, 22/2/1940.

7 Terence Brown, *Ireland: A Social and Cultural History, 1922 to the Present*, Cornell, 1981, p. 131.

8 *Irish Independent*, 2/12/1941.

9 The cost of living went up by 70 per cent in the period 1942–6. Diarmaid Ferriter, *The Transformation of Ireland: 1900–2000*, 2004, Profile Books, p. 383.

10 John Ryan, *Remembering How We Stood*, Lilliput Press, 2008, p. 14.

11 Maureen Diskin's account of the war in Dublin was published in Benjamin Grob-Fitzgibbon's *The Irish Experience during the Second World War: An Oral History*. It is anthologized in *Ireland: The Autobiography*, John Bowman (ed.), Penguin Ireland, 2016, p. 184.

12 Allison Maxwell and Shay Harpur, *Jammet's of Dublin 1901–1967*, Lilliput Press, 2011, p. 45.

13 Patrick Byrne made this point in an interview with the author.

14 Kevin C. Kearns, *Dublin Street Life & Lore*, Gill & Macmillan, 1991, p. 49.

15 *Irish Independent*, 6/7/1940.

16 Tim Carey, *Dublin since 1922*, Hachette, 2016, p. 136.

17 *Evening Mail*, 3/10/1940.

18 *Evening Mail*, 5/10/1940.

19 *Evening Mail*, 31/5/1941.

20 *People's Press*, 14/6/1941.

21 *Irish Independent*, 22/8/1942. The same report continues: 'What fascinated me most was the small heap of spoiled votes. I was amused by the almost Rabelaisian humour of some of the remarks or even verses scrawled over the papers. I liked best the gesture of the voter who had written his own name on the top of the ballot paper, then proceeding to vote only for himself.'

22 *Longford Leader*, 31/10/1942.

23 *Irish Press*, 5/12/1944.

24 *Irish Press*, 26/1/1945.

25 *Evening Herald*, 31/5/1944.

26 *Irish Independent*, 1/6/1944.

27 *Irish Press*, 5/9/1944.

28 'Everyone was living in poverty. On a Monday morning there'd be queues going up to the pawn . . . And we'd no gas, no light. The first man that got us electric light was Alfie Byrne, the old Lord Mayor of Dublin ten times. A great man. All the poor he looked after. If there was anyone down here in trouble he'd be down that night, in the 1930s and all.' Billy Dunleavy, quoted in Kevin C. Kearns, *Dublin Tenement Life: An Oral History*, Gill & Macmillan, 1994, p. 83.

29 Maureen O'Sullivan TD was responding to an article by the author in the *Sunday Times*, published 5/7/2015. Gerry Fay of the North Wall Community Association said that Tony Gregory was an admirer of Byrne. Fay also told the author that Byrne got Luke Kelly's family a house in Whitehall after their home in Lattimore Cottages was badly damaged in a fire.

30 *Irish Independent*, 9/5/1945.

31 *Irish Press*, 14/5/1945.

32 F. S. L. Lyons, *Ireland since the Famine*, Scribner, 1971, pp. 557–8.

33 Interview with Patrick Byrne, 18/5/2017.

16. Coldest Winter Ever

1 Byrne filed the letter after writing in the left-hand corner: 'Five pounds sent 19 March 47.' ABC.

2 Anthony Cronin, writing in *Magnum Ireland*, Val Williams and Brigitte Lardinois (eds.), Thames & Hudson, 2005, p. 17.

3 *Evening Herald*, 14/6/1946.

4 John P. Swift, writing in *James Larkin: Lion of the Fold*, Donal Nevin (ed.), Gill & Macmillan, 1998, p. 91.

5 Tim Carey, *Dublin since 1922*, Hachette, 2016, p. 145.

6 *J. P. Donleavy's Ireland*, 1986, quoted in the *Oxford Book of Ireland*, Patricia Craig (ed.), 1988, p. 35.

7 *Evening Herald*, 29/11/1945.

8 *Cork Examiner*, 12/3/1947.

9 *Irish Press*, 17/4/1947.

10 *Cork Examiner*, 29/8/1947. Byrne also remained upset about communism. His fear of it was not particularly helpful on the international stage. As the Dáil debated joining the United Nations, he worried about what it would mean for Irish neutrality. What would our position be 'if the Communist element got the upper hand in the Security Council and we were ordered to take part in an attack on some small oppressed country?' Inflammatory comments by the Russian Foreign Minister prompted him to demand that the Minister withdraw Ireland's application. And in due course the application was refused because of objections from the Soviet Union.

11 The Manager of the Masterpiece Cinema assured Byrne that money would not be an issue. 'I do not propose to make any charge.' 15/1/1948. ABC.

12 *Sunday Express*, 5/3/1961. There is also a bill from the Emerald Girl Piper' Band for 'services of the band during the recent election campaign . . . I trust that we carried out all the arrangements to your full satisfaction.' 17/2/1948. ABC.

13 Lyrics of 'Byrne for Dublin', ABC.

14 David McCullagh, *The Reluctant Taoiseach*, Gill Books, 2010, p. 8.

15 'Lord Mayor of Dublin, at Manchester'. Undated speech, ABC.

16 Letter from John Herron, 21/11/1948. ABC. Another correspondent wrote, 'I voted for the "Fine Gale" at the last election, an action which I deeply regret.'

17 *Cork Examiner*, 25/11/1948.

18 *Cork Examiner*, 26/11/1948.

19 Radio appeal made by Byrne on Radio Éireann, 8/11/1953. ABC.

20 Tim Carey, *Dublin since 1922*, op. cit., p. 166.

21 This anecdote is recalled in Patrick Maume's entry on Seán T. O'Kelly in the *Dictionary of Irish Biography*.

22 *Irish Independent*, 2/5/1952.

23 *Sunday Independent*, 11/10/2009.

24 Patrick Maume on Seán T. O'Kelly, op. cit.

25 *Cork Examiner*, 1/7/1952.

26 His funeral was attended by the Taoiseach, Éamon de Valera and the leader of the opposition, John A. Costello.

27 *Irish Independent*, 11/11/1952.

28 Letter from Mulcahy to Byrne, 1/6/1953. ABC.

29 The article continues, 'Referring to a statement in yesterday's *Evening Herald* to the effect that he had removed one of Ald. T. Byrne's election posters, Mr Colm Gallagher, T.D., told an *Irish Press* reporter that the poster in question was displayed within the precincts of a polling booth in the main hall of

St. Finbar's N.S. which was illegal, and that it was removed after consultation with the Gardai.'

30 Maurice Manning pointed out that Tom Byrne secured twice the Fianna Fáil vote in his book, *James Dillon: A Biography*, published by Wolfhound, 1999.

31 *Irish Press*, 20/11/1952.

32 Con O'Leary, 'Poor Man's Friend: The Story of Dublin's Lord Mayor', *Sunday Graphic and Sunday News*, 18/11/1934. ABC.

17. Alfred X

1 On 27 June 1955, Byrne wrote a reference: 'The bearer, Miss E. B. Gavin, is a personal friend of mine. She is Secretary to Mr Maurice E. Dockrell, T.D., one of my colleagues of the Corporation of Dublin and also a member of the Irish House of Parliament. Miss Gavin is on a visit to London and Paris and I will be deeply grateful for any consideration shown to her.'

2 Letter to Byrne from F. H. Doyle, 4/7/1954. ABC.

3 In December 1954, an ex-Garda superintendent sent his list of Christmas presents to an old man with white whiskers. Dublin still believed in Alfie Byrne: 'I am badly in need of some clothes and do excuse me if I am asking too much. I did some good work for some of those charitable organisations when I was with the Garda. I require very badly and urgently a suit of clothes, say a blue one with a stripe in it, an overcoat single breasted Raglan style, black hat to match say Anthony Eden style, socks. 10½ size under clothing vest and pants; white shirt for 16½ collar; pair of shoes mocassin, size 7½ very very wide, a waterproof coat and hand bag to put them in, also a pair of gloves size 8. I like to be respectfully dressed though I am only a pauper thanking you in anticipation, wishing you all

blessing compliments of the season.' Letter to Alfie Byrne, 7/12/1954. ABC.

4 Letter to Byrne from Bell Brothers Circus, 25/6/1954. ABC.

5 *Sunday Independent*, 27/2/1955. ABC.

6 Letter from Byrne to Master Raymond Doyle, Roscrea, Co. Tipperary, 29/7/1954. ABC.

7 Letter from Byrne to Lilli Austin, 5/4/1955. ABC.

8 In April 1931, the Mansion House hosted an exhibition of young painters, the Associated Irish Artists. The 140 paintings had been rejected by the prestigious Royal Hibernian Academy. Space was found in the Mansion House because, said Byrne, he felt sorry for these mavericks, who resented what they called the 'autocratic methods' of the RHA. 'That was strong language, was it not?' said Byrne.

9 Letter to Byrne, 4/10/1954. ABC.

10 Interview with Michael O'Halloran, former Lord Mayor of Dublin, 4/3/2017.

11 Letter from Byrne to Councillor Charles J. Haughey, B.Comm., BL, ACA, 17 Ideal Homes Estate, Howth Road, Raheny. 17/12/1954. ABC.

12 Letter to Byrne from US Navy Captain Henry J. Armstrong, USS *Worcester*, 13/12/1954. ABC.

13 Eamon Dunphy, *The Rocky Road*, Penguin, 2013, p. 30.

14 *Cork Examiner*, 16/3/1956.

15 In 1942, McQuaid advised an English bishop to decline an honorary degree from Trinity: 'Your action in accepting the degree will tend to make still more difficult the execution of the existing law of the Maynooth Synod by which Catholics may not enter Trinity College.' John Cooney, *John Charles McQuaid: Ruler of Catholic Ireland*, O'Brien Press, 1999, p. 162.

16 *Evening Mail*, 5/7/1955. ABC.

17 Unknown and undated newspaper clipping. ABC.

18 Menu for Patrick J. Hernon's retirement dinner. ABC.

19 *Evening Herald*, 15/3/1956.

20 *Manchester Guardian*, 15/3/1956.

21 Telegrams arrived from many places, including one from the Mayor of New York, Robert F. Wagner. 'Alderman Byrne had attained high office of Lord Mayor many times, but he never lost contact with the poor and the underprivileged, whose champion he was.' When Wagner visited Ireland in 1955, he told the papers, 'I do want to shake the hand of Alfie Byrne.'

22 *People*, 18/3/1956.

23 *Irish Times*, 16/3/1956.

Epilogue: Whatever Happened to Alfie Byrne?

1 Quoted by David Dickson in *Dublin: The Making of a Capital City*, Profile Books, 2014, p. 1.

2 *Daily Express*, 29/6/1937.

Bibliography

Official publications

Report of Parliamentary Debates Vol. LXXXV (1916)
Report of Parliamentary Debates Vol. LXXXVI (1916)
Report of Parliamentary Debates Vol. XC (1917)
Dáil Éireann debates (1922–56)

Newspapers, periodicals and journals

American New York
Anglo-Celt
An Phoblacht
Atlantic
Belfast Newsletter
Belfast Telegraph
Birmingham Mail
Birmingham Post
Boston Evening Transcript
Boston Herald
Catholic Herald
Catholic Mind
Church of Ireland Gazette
Connaught Tribune
Cork Examiner
Daily Express
Daily Herald
Daily Mail
Daily Mirror

Daily Sketch
Daily Telegraph
Denbighshire Free Press
Derry Journal
Derry People
Donegal News
Drogheda Argus
Dublin Opinion
Dubliner
Economic and
   Social Review
Edinburgh Evening Dispatch
Evening Herald
Evening Mail
Evening Standard
Fermanagh Herald
Frontier Sentinel
Freeman's Journal
Gazette and Daily

Glasgow Herald
History Ireland
Irish Examiner
Irish Independent
Irish Press Cutting Agency
Irish Press
Irish Times
Isle of Man Times
Journal
Kerry News
Leeds Mercury
Leitrim Observer
Limerick Leader
Liverpool Echo
Liverpool Post
London Evening Standard
Longford Leader
Manchester Guardian
Midland Tribune
Morning Advertiser
Morning Post
New Era Lancaster
News Review
New York Daily Mirror
New York World Telegram

Northern Whig
Offaly Chronicle
Pathé Gazette
People
People's Press
Roscommon Herald
Saturday Herald
Southern Star
Strabane Chronicle
Sunday Chronicle
Sunday Dispatch
Sunday Express
Sunday Graphic and Sunday News
Sunday Independent
Sunderland Echo
Times (London)
Times (New York)
Times (Sunday)
Tipperary Star
Truth
Waterford Star
Wicklow People
World Telegram
Yorkshire Post

Books

Banville, John, *Magnum Ireland* (London, 2005)
Bartlett, Thomas, *Ireland: A History* (Cambridge, 2014)
Bowman, John, *Ireland: The Autobiography* (London, 2016)

Brown, Terence, *Ireland: A Social and Cultural History, 1922 to the Present* (Cornell, 1981)

Bunbury, Turtle, *The Glorious Madness – Tales of the Irish and the Great War* (Dublin, 2014)

Callanan, Frank, 'Dillon, John', *Dictionary of Irish Biography* (Dublin and Cambridge, 2009)

Carden, Sheila, *Alderman Tom Kelly and Dublin Corporation* (Dublin, 2007)

Carey, Tim, *Dublin since 1922* (Dublin, 2016)

Clark, Mary, *The Dublin Civic Portrait Collection: Patronage, Politics and Patriotism 1603–2013* (Dublin, 2016)

Coleman, Marie, *The Irish Sweep* (Dublin, 2009)

Cooney, John, *John Charles McQuaid: Ruler of Catholic Ireland* (Dublin, 1999)

Corless, Damien, *You'll Ruin Your Dinner: Sweet Memories from Irish Childhood* (Dublin, 2012)

Costello, Peter, 'Joyce, James', *Dictionary of Irish Biography* (Dublin and Cambridge, 2009)

Craig, Patricia P., 'Donleavy's Ireland, 1986', *Oxford Book of Ireland* (New York, 1998)

Cronin, Anthony, *Dead as Doornails* (Dublin, 1976)

—, *Magnum Ireland*, Val Williams & Brigitte Lardinois (eds.) (London, 2005)

Cronin, Mike, *The Blueshirts and Irish Politics* (Dublin, 1997)

Cullen, Bill, *It's a Long Way from Penny Apples* (Dublin, 2002)

Curran, Michael J., 'Witness statement', Bureau of Military History Collection 1913–21

Daly, Mary E., *Social and Economic History of Ireland since 1800* (Dublin, 1981)

Dempsey, Pauric J., 'Belton, Patrick', *Dictionary of Irish Biography* (Dublin and Cambridge, 2009)

Dickson, *David, Dublin: The Making of a Capital City* (London, 2014)

Dolan, Anne, 'Byrne, Alfred (Alfie)', *Dictionary of Irish Biography* (Dublin and Cambridge, 2009)

Dolan, Terence Patrick, *A Dictionary of Hiberno-English: The Irish Use of English* (Dublin, 2006)

Dunphy, Eamon, *The Rocky Road* (Dublin, 2013)

Fallon, Donal, *The Pillar: The Life and Afterlife of the Nelson Pillar* (Dublin, 2014)

Fanning, Ronan, *Independent Ireland* (Dublin, 1983)

Ferriter, Diarmaid, *Judging Dev: A Reassessment of the Life and Legacy of Éamon de Valera* (Dublin, 2007)

—, *Occasions of Sin: Sex and Society in Modern Ireland* (London, 2009)

—, *The Transformation of Ireland 1900–2000* (London, 2004)

Foster, R. F., *Modern Ireland, 1600–1972* (London, 1989)

—, *Vivid Faces: The Revolutionary Generation in Ireland, 1890–1923* (Dublin, 2015)

Friedman, Alan Warren, *Fictional Death and the Modernist Enterprise* (Cambridge, 1995)

Garvin, Tom, 'Irish Voters and Irish Political Development: A Comparative Perspective', *Economic and Social Research Institute, Economic and Social Review*, Vol. 8, No. 3, 1977, pp. 161–86

Gifford, Don, *Joyce Annotated* (Oakland, 1982)

Hart, Peter, *Mick: The Real Michael Collins* (New York, 2007)

Joyce, James, *Finnegans Wake* (London, 1939)

—, *Letters of James Joyce*, Stuart Gilbert & Richard Ellmann (eds.), Vols. 2 & 3 (London, 1966)

—, *The Selected Letters of James Joyce*, Richard Ellmann (ed.) (London, 1975)

Joyce, Stanislaus, *My Brother's Keeper: James Joyce's Early Years*, Richard Ellmann (ed.) (Boston, 1958)

Kearns, George P. & Patrick Maguire, *A to Z of All Old Dublin Cinemas* (Dublin, 2006)

Kearns, Kevin C., *Dublin Street Life and Lore* (Dublin, 1991)

—, *Dublin Tenement Life: An Oral History* (Dublin, 1994)

Kee, Robert, *Ireland: A History* (London, 2003)

Keogh, Dermot, *Twentieth-century Ireland: Revolution and State Building* (Dublin, 2005)

Kelly, Alderman Thomas, *The Streets of Dublin, 1910–1911*, Dublin Civic Trust (Dublin, 2013)

Kiberd, Declan, 'Irish Literature and Irish History', *Oxford History of Ireland*, R. F. Foster (ed.) (Oxford, 2001)

Laffan, Michael, 'Cosgrave, William Thomas', *Dictionary of Irish Biography* (Dublin and Cambridge, 2009)

—, *Judging W. T. Cosgrave* (Dublin, 2014)

—, *The Resurrection of Ireland: The Sinn Féin Party, 1916–1923* (Cambridge, 1999)

Lawless, Colonel Joseph V., 'Recollections of the Anglo-Irish War: 1915–1921', Bureau of Military History Collection 1913–1921

Leahy, Thomas, 'Witness statement', Bureau of Military History Collection 1913–1921

Long, Patrick, 'O'Duffy, Eoin', *Dictionary of Irish Biography* (Dublin and Cambridge, 2009)

Lyon, Anne, *Constitutional History of the UK* (London, 2003)

Lyons, F. S. L., *John Dillon: A Biography* (London, 1968)

—, *The Irish Parliamentary Party, 1890–1910* (London, 1951)

Manning, Maurice, *The Blueshirts* (Dublin, 1970)

—, *James Dillon: A Biography* (Dublin, 1999)

Marreco, Anne, *The Rebel Countess: The Life and Times of Constance Markievicz* (London, 2000)

Maume, Patrick, 'O'Kelly, Séan Thomas', *Dictionary of Irish Biography* (Dublin and Cambridge, 2009)

Maxwell, Allison & Shay Harpur, *Jammet's of Dublin 1901–1967* (Dublin, 2011)

McCoole, Sinéad, *Passion and Politics: Sir John Lavery – The Salon Revisited* (Dublin, 2010)

McCullagh, David, *The Reluctant Taoiseach* (Dublin, 2010)

McEllin, David, 'Legendary Lord Mayor Alfie Byrne', *Leaders of the City, Dublin's First Citizens, 1500–1950*, Ruth McManus & Lisa-Marie Griffith (eds.), (Dublin, 2013)

McGarry, Fearghal, *Eoin O'Duffy: A Self-made Hero* (Oxford, 2005)

—, *Irish Politics and the Spanish Civil War* (Cork, 1999)

—, *The Abbey Rebels of 1916* (Dublin, 2015)

McManus, Ruth & Lisa-Marie Griffith (eds.), *Leaders of the City: Dublin's First Citizens, 1500–1950* (Dublin, 2013)

Meehan, Ciara, *The Cosgrave Party: A History of Cumann Na nGaedheal, 1923–33* (Dublin, 2010)

Morrissey, Thomas J., *Laurence O'Neill: Patriot and Man of Peace* (Dublin, 2014)

Mulvagh, Conor, *The Irish Parliamentary Party at Westminster, 1900–1918* (Manchester, 2016)

Murphy, Brian, *Forgotten Patriot: Douglas Hyde and the Foundation of the Irish Presidency* (Dublin, 2016)

Nevin, Donal (ed.), *James Larkin: Lion of the Fold* (Dublin, 2006)

Perolz, Marie, 'Witness statement', Bureau of Military History Collection 1913–1921

O'Brien, Marie & Conor Cruise O'Brien, *Concise History of Ireland* (London, 1988)

O'Casey, Séan, *Autobiographies II: Innisfallen, Fare Thee Well, Rose and Crown, and Sunset and Evening Star* (London, 1963)

O'Halpin, Eunan, 'Cosgrave, William Thomas', *Dictionary of Irish Biography* (Dublin and Cambridge, 2009)

O'Riordain, Michael, *Connolly Column: The Story of the Irishmen Who Fought for the Spanish Republic, 1936–39* (Dublin, 1979)

Rockett, Kevin, *Irish Film Censorship* (Dublin, 2004)

Rowley, Ellen Catherine (ed.), *More than Concrete Blocks: Dublin City's Twentieth-century Buildings and Their Stories, 1900–1940*, Vol. 1 (Dublin, 2016)

Ryan, John, *Remembering How We Stood: Bohemian Dublin at the Mid-century* (Dublin, 1975)

Sheehan, Ronan and Brendan Walsh, *Dublin: The Heart of the City* (Dublin, 1988)

Valiulis, Maryann Gialanella, *Portrait of a Revolutionary: General Richard Mulcahy and the Founding of the Irish Free State* (Lexington, 1992)

Waldron, Fionnuala, 'Defending the Cause: Parnell and the Drink Interest', *Parnell Reconsidered*, Pauric Travers & Donal McCartney (eds.) (Dublin, 2013)

Wyse Jackson, John, *Dublin: A Collection of the Poetry of Place* (London, 2009)

Yeates, Padraig, *A City in Turmoil: Dublin 1919–1921* (Dublin, 2012)

—, *A City in Wartime, Dublin 1914–18* (Dublin, 2011)

—, *Lockout: Dublin 1913* (Dublin, 2000)

Yeats, W. B., *Michael Robartes and the Dancer* (Dublin, 1921)

Index